AMERICA'S SONG

The YANKEY's return from CAMP.

FATHER and I went down to camp,
  Along with Captain Gooding,
There we see the men and boys,
  As thick as hasty-pudding.
    Yankey doodle keep it up,
Chorus. Yankey doodle, dandy,
    Mind the music and the step,
    And with the girls be handy.
And there we see a thousand men,
  As rich as 'Squire David ;
And what they wasted every day,
  I wish it could be saved.
    Yankey doodle, &c.
The 'lasses they eat every day,
  Would keep a house a winter :
They have as much that I'll be bound
  They eat it when they're a mind to.
    Yankey doodle, &c.
And there we see a swamping gun,
  Large as a log of maple,
Upon a ducid little cart,
  A load for father's cattle.
    Yankey doodle. &c.
And every time they shoot it off,
  It takes a horn of powder—
It makes a noise like father's gun,
  Only a nation louder.
    Yankey doodle, &c.
I went as nigh to one myself,
  As 'Siah's underpining ;
And father went as nigh again,
  I tho't the deuce was in him.
    Yankey doodle, &c.
Cousin Simon grew so bold,
  I tho't he would have cock'd it :
It scar'd me so, I shrink'd it off,
  And hung by father's pocket.
    Yankey doodle, &c.
And captain Davis had a gun,
  He kind of clapt his hand on't,

And stuck a crooked stabbing iron
  Upon the little end on't.
    Yankey doodle, &c.
And there I see a pumpkin shell
  as big as mother's bason,
And ev'ry time they touch'd it off,
  They scamper'd like the nation.
    Yankey doodle, &c.
I see a little barrel too,
  The heads were made of leather,
They knock'd upon't with little clubs,
  and call'd the folks together.
    Yankey doodle, &c.
And there was captain Washington,
  and gentlefolks about him,
They say he's grown so tarnal proud,
  He will not ride without 'em.
    Yankey doodle, &c.
He got him on his meeting clothes,
  Upon a slapping stallion,
He set the world along in rows,
  In hundreds and in millions.
    Yankey doodle, &c.
The flaming ribbons in their hats,
  They look'd so taring fine, ah,
wanted pockily to get,
  To give to my Jemimah.
    Yankey doodle, &c.
I see another snarl of men
  a digging graves, they told me,
So tarnal long, so tarnal deep,
  They 'tended they should hold me.
    Yankey doodle, &c.
It scar'd me so, I hook'd it off,
  Nor stop'd, as I remember,
Nor turn'd about 'till I got home,
  Lock'd up in mother's chamber.
    Yankey doodle, &c.

An early broadside with "Yankee Doodle" verses that became the accepted version and were published in at least three broadsides, printed and distributed in the United States and England late in the eighteenth century.

AMERICA'S SONG

The Story of 'Yankee Doodle'

STUART MURRAY

IMAGES FROM THE PAST

BENNINGTON, VERMONT

By arrangement with
Marian and Robert Guerriero

Cover: "Yankee Doodle, or a Fourth of July Celebration" was the title Ohio artist Archibald M. Willard first gave his early concept for "The Spirit of '76," which was first painted in 1876; the model for the central figure was Willard's father, a native Vermonter whose father — a Green Mountain Boy — had been present at Burgoyne's surrender in 1777. This version of the painting dates from 1895.

1 2 3 4 5 6 7 8 9 10 XXX 06 05 04 03 02 01 00 99

Library of Congress Cataloging-in-Publication Data
Murray, Stuart, 1948-
  America's Song: The Story of Yankee Doodle/by Stuart Murray.
  p.   cm.
  Includes bibliographical references and index.
  ISBN 1-884592-18-X (cloth)
  1. Yankee Doodle (Song) 2. Title.
  ML3561.Y2 M87   1999
  782.42'1599'0973 – dc21

                                                    99-30294
                                                    CIP

Copyright© 1999 Stuart Murray
Published by Images from the Past, Inc.,
P.O. Box 137, Bennington, VT 05201
Tordis Ilg Isselhardt, Publisher

Printed in the United States of America

Design and Production: Ron Toelke Associates, Chatham, NY
Printer: Thomson-Shore, Inc., Dexter, MI
Text and Display: Adobe Caslon
Paper: 55lb. Glatfelter Supple Opaque Recycled Natural
Cover: 12pt.C1S

JONATHAN: *No, no, I can sing no more. Some other time, when you and I are better acquainted, I'll sing the whole of it — no, no — that's a fib — I can't sing but a hundred and ninety-nine verses: Our Tabitha at home can sing it all —*

From the play *The Contrast* by Royall Tyler, which premiered in 1787 in New York; Jonathan, the first "stage Yankee," has been singing "Yankee Doodle."

To the Bailey family:

Henry, Chip, Marilyn,
Johnny, Lisa, and Hank

CONTENTS

YANKEE DOODLE
Arr.: John Philip Sousa

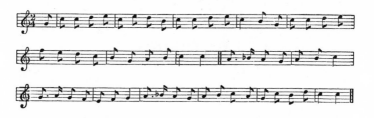

OUR SONG

Where does an ancient melody come from? Passed down through the centuries, a much-loved old tune is given new words, new meaning, new life. It links generation after generation to those who sang and played it long before, who gave it words and made it their own.

The origins of "Yankee Doodle," perhaps the most familiar tune in all the world, are lost in the distant past. Scholars can only speculate on how America's famous national air came to be and why, in colonial days, it stirred up such powerful emotions. Some of their scholarship is offered in the second part of this book, "The Study," as is the history behind the first part — "The Story" of America's song.

"Yankee Doodle" has appeared in many versions down the centuries. This is mine.

Stuart Murray
East Chatham, New York

In service of Dutch merchants, English navigator Henry Hudson sails his ship Half Moon *in the lower reaches of the river that one day would bear his name.*

Prologue

HUDSON'S RIVER

IN THE AUTUMN OF 1609, the Dutch carrack *Halve Maen*, under the command of English navigator Henry Hudson, sailed into the mouth of a great unexplored river on the coast of North America in search of a northwest passage to the Orient.

The eighty-ton *Half Moon* sailed upriver, past looming cliffs on the left and an island on the right, where there were native villages that sent out light canoes to greet the strangers. From that island wafted the fragrance of sweet grasses and wild flowers, and Hudson saw on a map made by another Englishman who had been here in 1607 that it bore the name "Manahatin." This apparently was the name the native people gave the island, but it was of little interest to Hudson, who had not been hired by the Dutch merchants to dally at lovely islands. Escorted by canoes and trading with the natives as he went, he journeyed northward on the river, urgently, wearily, seeking an outlet to the western seas and China. He found none and turned around to sail downriver and back to the Netherlands and the merchants who had sent him out.

A disappointed Englishman and a Dutch ship in search of a fabled passage to the Orient began the argument over the right to colonize this country — an argument that would rage for another half century: did Hudson's exploration of the river that one day would bear his name give rights of discovery to the Dutch who employed him or to the English who were his own people? Soon after Hudson's return, both nations claimed by right of discovery the river valley and the tributaries that flowed into it, and likewise claimed the northeastern coastline he visited on the voyage, which otherwise was considered something of a failure.

In the years that followed, Dutch fur traders arrived in the river and began a lucrative enterprise that could make them a fortune in one hard-working season living among the Indians. With the permission of the natives, small Dutch settlements followed, one at the river's head of navigation and one on the island called Manahatin. At the same time, the English were settling large colonies to the east. While a handful of Dutch traders came and went on the great river, pursuing Indian furs at the northern reaches and offering a safe harbor for seagoing shipping at the river's mouth, thousands of English were founding plantations — agricultural and fishing colonies — in a new world that to them was their own Promised Land.

At first the Dutch in New Netherland and the English in

New England were friends, for their nations once had been allies in war against the mighty Spanish, and they had won. In time, however, their interests in America began to conflict, for New England could not hold its colonists, who were ambitious and restless and wanted to possess the rich lands of the Hudson and Delaware rivers. It made the New Englanders all the more hungry to see that the sketchy rule of thinly populated New Netherland was all that stood in their way.

They were much alike, the Dutch and English of the 1600s, and knew each other well, but they were uneasy neighbors in the new land, which both believed was theirs by right of discovery and by the hand of their god. Three generations after Hudson's voyage, the issue would be decided by force of arms, and the Dutch of New Netherland would be overwhelmed. Their legacy would be taken up and overlaid by the English so that the Dutch heritage in the New World was almost forgotten — even all those things that were Dutch long before they were English or American, and even a name the Dutch gave the English as an insult.

A name that became part of a lighthearted song, which one day became all of America's song.

The emblem of New Netherland, with the fur-bearing beaver at the center.

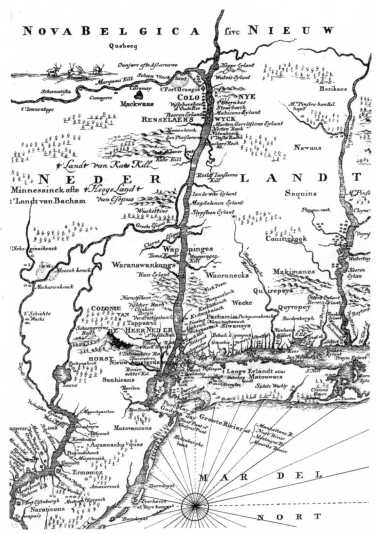

A map of New Netherland in 1656.

PART I

The Story

One

NEW NETHERLAND AND NEW ENGLAND

Thierry…thinks our etymologies of the word Yankee are all wrong, and that, having arisen from the collision and jeerings of the Dutch and the English in New York and New England, it is from the Dutch Jan — pronounced Yan — with the very common diminutive kee.…

George Ticknor, 1838, in his *Life, Letters, and Journals.*

Though sometimes dragged into the discussion, the derivation of the word 'Yankee' evidently furnishes no tangible clue to the origin of the song 'Yankee Doodle.'

Oscar G. Sonneck, first head of the Music Division of the Library of Congress, in his 1909 research report on the origin of "Yankee Doodle."

A N ATLANTIC BREEZE BLEW ACROSS the Dutch fields of Long Island, stirring the yellow grain where reapers scythed and stacked the harvest on this hot day in August 1664. Blades sliced and hands bundled and the folk joined in a cheerful old-country tune that encouraged everyone to work together. Wearing colorful shirts and broad-brimmed hats, the reapers sang louder whenever they came to the song's refrain, mostly nonsense words:

> *Jonker, didle, doedel, down*
> *Didel, doedel, landheer,*
> *Jonker, viver, voover, vown,*
> *Botermelk en tanther.*

Everyone in the colony of New Netherland knew this song and always had, although the refrain's original meaning had been forgotten long ago. In Dutch, *jonker* (pronounced "yonker") meant a country squire, and the jonker in the song was a *doedel* (pronounced "doodle"), a simpleton or fool. Other words recalled how jonkers often paid their laborers with buttermilk, *botermelk*, and one-tenth of the laborer's harvest, a *tanther*. The Dutch West India Company, which managed New Netherland, also dealt in tanthers — charging its farmers a tenth of their production as a fee for renting company lands.

While they worked here in the grain fields of *Middelwout* (Midwood), the New Netherland harvesters made up their own verses to the jonker doodle tune. The jonker's silliness was a favorite theme, and in English, one might go like this:

Jonker doodle came to town
In his stripèd trousers,
Couldn't see the town because
There were so many houses.

Most colonists in New Netherland, like these at Middelwout, worked for the Company, and few could afford to own their own farms. Not so with the hundreds of prosperous settlers who had migrated to Long Island from New England and bought farms here. The first settlers from New England were seeking religious freedom, which they were not allowed in their Puritan-dominated home colonies. It was said that New Netherland had been populated largely because of New England's religious tyranny, which had driven many of its people to seek liberty in the Dutch colony. The iron-fisted laws of New Haven and Hartford forbade even freedom of thinking, but in New Netherland a man could mind his own business and be left alone with his faith and private thoughts.

Then more New England settlers had come to Long Island, but these were devout Puritans who were after the good land and mild climate. They had flourished, even establishing their own villages, until more than a dozen English villages grew up over the length of the island. There were only five Dutch villages on Long Island, all of them here on the western end, a few miles from the port of New Amsterdam. The Dutch West India

Company, based in old Amsterdam, was willing to sell land to New Englanders, but it had done little to promote settlement from Holland. The Company was mainly interested in profits from the colony's fur trade, so it had not encouraged Dutch farmers to come over and plant communities of permanent settlers.

New Amsterdam was first and foremost a Company town, a trading port, where furs, timber, and grain were shipped, and where vessels put in for supplies and paid the Company dearly for harbor fees. The lords of the Company liked it that way and were not about to trouble themselves with developing a thriving Dutch colony. The Dutch-owned Long Island farms like this one at Middelwout were bountiful, but few in number compared to those of the English.

When trumpet blasts rang out across the Middelwout grain fields, the harvesters stopped singing to look toward the road. By now, this fanfare was a familiar sound to the harvesters, who had heard it all summer long — the blare of trumpets announced once again the comings and goings of John Winthrop, Jr., governor of the newly established colony of Connecticut. Winthrop had been visiting English settlers on eastern Long Island, which his colony controlled; but now he often came to the New Netherland end of the island to meet with the English residents, many of whom wanted him to annex their towns to Connecticut.

With every passing year, relations between the English and Dutch colonies had worsened, and it was no wonder, because New Netherland claimed much of New England, and New

England claimed all New Netherland, which originally had stretched from the Connecticut River west to the Delaware. Twelve thousand New Netherlanders, who were scattered from Long Island northward to the Mohawk River and southward to Chesapeake Bay, could never hope to hold their colony against the New Englanders with their burgeoning population of more than forty thousand.

By now, the "English Johnnies" as the New Netherlanders

John Winthrop, Jr., governor of the colony of Hartford and later of all Connecticut, intended to eliminate New Netherland and take control of its territory, which stretched from the Connecticut River to the Delaware.

called them — *Engelse Jankes* in Dutch — were determined to sweep away Holland's rule at New Amsterdam and open up the rich and beautiful country of New Netherland to their own kind. The Jankes, pronounced "Yahn-kes," who had colonized the Connecticut River valley had driven out the Dutch there and then had come over to settle on Dutch Long Island. They also had migrated just north of New Amsterdam in a place the Dutch called East Village (*Oostdorp*), but which the Jankes called Westchester. At first the English who came to live in New Netherland had sworn allegiance to the Dutch government and the Dutch West India Company, but that all had changed.

Now, here was the grim Governor Winthrop of Connecticut brazenly riding across territory that belonged to New Netherland, leading a column of armed Puritans in tall hats and long cloaks, some with chest armor and iron helmets, many carrying muskets and pikes. As the Dutch harvesters watched the passing of that column, it was a reminder that five years ago the Company had signed a treaty with the New England colonies, giving up the eastern half of the island because New Netherland did not have the strength to make war with them. The Dutch West India Company wanted profit from America, not war. On this summer day, Winthrop and his Janken retinue well knew there were no Dutch fighting men to oppose them, especially since so many had been sent up the North River to deal with Indian troubles. Furthermore, the outnumbered Dutch on Long Island feared their families, homes, and crops would be endangered if they mustered to fight the Jankes. Winthrop was organizing the English living on Long Island and was laying the groundwork for its final annexation to New England.

The English on the island could put more men under arms than could "Old Silvernails" — peg-legged Pieter Stuyvesant, the Dutch director-general who ruled from New Amsterdam. Stuyvesant was a hard and warlike character determined to defend the rights of the Company that employed him, but he could not dictate to the English settlers the Company had allowed to come to Long Island. When some had risen up in rebellion a year ago, defiantly placing themselves under the protection of Winthrop and the arrogant Jankes, Stuyvesant could do nothing to oppose them. The rebels had bluntly warned that anyone who stood in their way would face fire and sword.

To New Netherlanders, the Puritan Jankes of New England could be unbelievably hardhearted. Some years ago, when New England families who had fled to New Netherland in search of religious freedom were massacred by Indians, the Puritans had looked heavenward, saying coldly that it was a "heavy example" of God's hand punishing those who had gone to live in the hotbed of sin that was New Netherland. Indeed, compared to pious-minded New England, with its sacred quest to make the most of their Promised Land, New Netherland was a money-minded Sodom, a hodgepodge of faiths and cultures.

The Dutch colony had as many religions as it did languages — eighteen languages by one count. The official religion was Dutch Calvinism, practiced by Hollanders and by French-speaking Walloons from Belgium, but the people were allowed to worship in their own way as long as it was in their homes and not done in public. There were Lutherans from Germany and Norway; Anabaptists from Friesland; Catholics from England, Ireland, Italy, and Poland; Jews from Portugal, and a Moslem Turk or two; even Quakers were left alone if they did not openly proselytize. Among the English who had come to live in New Netherland most practiced their own personal brand of Puritanism; called Independents, they were dedicated to reforming the Church of England.

New Amsterdam, the colonial capital, was a key port lying on the triangular merchant route from the Caribbean to Europe and Africa. The town's three thousand inhabitants had their eighteen languages, and like the farm workers of Dutch Long Island were of almost every people, every race. The town swirled with fur traders and sailors, and many an enterprising homemaker kept a lively tavern. Often, New Amsterdam was mobbed with rowdy, unattached young men from ship crews and timber boats — men who liked to drink and sing and wench, and whose brawls tumbled into the streets, where they fought with knives. To keep the peace, Stuyvesant had ordered the taverns to close up by nine in the evening, when all beer taps were to be turned off, "taps put to," and the city's night watch drummed out a warning "tap-to" signal.

These footloose men often could find work in the grain fields, where the harvesters included off-duty soldiers in need of a day's pay and freebooting mulatto adventurers whose ship was laid up in dry dock; or perhaps a work gang of Angolan slaves was there, hired out by their owner, who might recently have fled the surrender of some Dutch colony in South America. The workers reaping the harvest near Middelwout included whites and blacks, freedmen and bondsmen, indentured servants, slaves, Indians, and hired hands — laboring for the farm owner and his family, who sweated alongside them.

At harvest time women and children worked, too. With their gaily colored skirts and half-bare legs, hair plaited boldly down their backs, and wearing the large earrings for which they were so well known, the women of New Netherland were proud and independent. They had rights under Dutch law that made them legally the match of men in most matters. New Netherland was the direct opposite of one-peopled, one-souled New England with its plain clothing, its harsh denial of the flesh, and severe regulations restricting singing and dancing or any show of ostentation.

It was a natural animosity. The Puritan colonies had been established around the same time as New Netherland, and there had always been conflict over who owned what lands, who had the right to the rich fur trade with the Indians, whose charter from their home government was legitimate. The Dutch and English even accused each other of stirring up the Indians to attack the other's settlers.

The ways of the New England Jankes could dismay the Dutch, especially when the Puritans persecuted women as witches and executed some. The madness of the witch hunts swept New England, but no one in New Netherland had been

Pieter Stuyvesant, for seventeen years director-general of New Netherland, a doomed colony of the Dutch West India Company.

harmed. It had come as a shock recently when Stuyvesant's own sister-in-law, who had married an Englishman and lived in New England, had been accused of witchcraft. Only the director-general's desperate personal intercession with highly placed acquaintances among the Puritan leaders had saved her life. Undeniably, the case might have been contrived as a way to torment Stuyvesant, the indomitable bulwark holding New Netherland against the encroachment of the New Englanders.

In 1654, when there had been worldwide war between England and Holland, an English fleet had come to America, about to pounce on New Amsterdam, but news of the treaty to end the war had arrived to prevent it. Now, ten years later, there was more trouble brewing between the home governments, and no one in New Netherland knew what to expect next. With all this militant movement of Winthrop and his dark-clothed, armed followers, however, it was obvious that the Dutch colony's existence hung on a thread.

Still, though there were worries, folk had to bring in the bounty of the fields at harvest time while the sun shone. Singing made the work easier — and also teased the sober Puritans with Winthrop. In a barn near the Middelwout fields, young people of all ages husked corn, stripping away leaves and corn silk and tossing the ears into a cart to be taken away by the older boys, then scorched before being ground into flour.

As they worked, they sang other verses to the old harvest melody.

Corn stalks, twist their hair off,
Cart wheels all around them,
Great wagons carry them off,
And mortar pestles pound them.

Corn stalks, twist your hair off,
Cart wheel frolic 'round you,
Fiery dragons take you off
And mortar's pestle pound you.

Some of the older boys dared sing the more risqué verses about the joyful celebrations at end of harvest time and the intoxicating round of parties and dancing that always followed completion of the work.

Now, when husking time is o'er,
They have a deucèd frolic,
There'll be some as drunk as sots,
The rest will have the colic.

It was not a verse for Puritan Jankes.

As the harvesters turned away from the passing of the hated Winthrop and his soldiers, it was simple enough to change the harvest song's "Jonker doedel" to "Janke doedel," and to make up verses about those fools of Connecticut Johnnies who were bent on taking over all New Netherland once they had the military might to do it. The Dutch even had a few more meanings for

As New Netherland civilians and mercenary soldiers look on, English warships enter the Hudson River during their invasion in 1664.

"Jan doedel," who could also be the town drunk, John the Fool; and a glass of gin was known as a "Jan doedel." Puritans did not drink gin, of course, but some of the more inquisitive ones were known to secretly visit New Amsterdam from time to time and partake of the bright lights and taverns. There was also the Dutch word *janker*, which signifies a howling cur, a yelper, growler, a complaining person, or worse, a dog. The New Netherlanders could mispronounce "Janke" as "janker," meaning a howling cur.

So the harvesters in these fields near Middelwout had more than one way to sing their "Jonker didel doedel" tune, but on this day the Connecticut Jankes were more dangerous than foolish doodles, for word came that Winthrop was meeting an English war fleet that had entered Nayack Bay, near Coney Island.

The crisis was upon them at last.

The New Englanders and their English cousins intended to march on New Amsterdam. Within hours, four hundred heavily armed English soldiers had disembarked from the ships and crowded into the muddy, narrow streets of the village of Gravesend. Already, the English settlers from Long Island were mustering their militia companies to join the soldiers and attack Stuyvesant.

The harvesters of Middelwout could only look on in dismay as the drums began to beat, and many a Janken was heard to boast that they would take New Amsterdam within days and then pillage and loot the city of all it was worth.

When the alarm about the English fleet at Nayack Bay reached New Amsterdam that August day, Director-general Stuyvesant had just hurried back to the city. He had been on an expedition for some weeks up the North River to neutralize a threat from the Indians near the Dutch town of Esopus. Stuyvesant had well known about the English royal fleet's presence in American waters and most recently at Boston, but he had been compelled to meet the threatened Indian uprising. By showing the tribes armed force, he had dissuaded them from moving against the settlers along the Esopus Creek. Now he had brought back his hundred or so soldiers and also had sent word to the more northerly settlements at Fort Orange asking them to release what men they could spare to meet the English invasion. Pieter Stuyvesant was a fighting man, a stubborn Frieslander undaunted by this far superior enemy force, just as he had been undaunted when a Spanish cannonball took off his leg in a colonial war many years ago.

By ten days after the arrival of the English fleet off Gravesend, Stuyvesant had done all he could to ready the city for a siege. Now he stumped along the grassy embankment of small Fort Amsterdam with its few old cannon placed on the Battery. He was a tall man, seeming even taller in his high-crowned hat and flowing cape, strong and agile at sixty-two years of age. With the silver nails of his peg leg glittering in the hot summer sun, he paced the rampart and looked down at the men working with shovel and pick to repair and strengthen the earthworks. Soldiers, slaves, and free burghers worked shoulder to shoulder to repair years of erosion and to lay down timbers that would deflect cannonballs from the English ships.

The defenders of New Amsterdam were few, and there was not enough food stockpiled to hold out more than a week or two, but that was all Stuyvesant had — that and his own courage, which was indomitable. He fully intended to resist the English, but not because he so loved the Dutch West India Company to which he had given such faithful service all these difficult years. No, the Company had let him down too often, had left him to manage a far-flung colony with too few resources to do it with. Stuyvesant would fight the English because he was a soldier with a soldier's honor and courage. A show of bravado might make the English think twice about launching a full-scale attack that would result in much bloodshed on both sides. Some well-placed cannonballs could sufficiently damage English warships to dampen their enthusiasm for a decisive artillery duel.

Scores of New Amsterdammers were hurriedly rebuilding the half-rotted palisade wall that Stuyvesant had erected in 1654 to defend the land approaches to the city. That had been the last time an attack by New England Jankes was threatening, but it had never come because the Massachusetts Bay and Plymouth colonies resisted the aggressive schemes of New Haven and Hartford. Massachusetts and Plymouth colonists had remembered better times, when Puritan Pilgrims had been taken in by the Dutch after the English king had persecuted them and driven them from their homeland in 1608, more than fifty years ago.

New Amsterdam seen from the Hudson River in the late 1660s; the fort is left of center, with the double-roofed Church of St. Nicholas.

The Pilgrims had lived for years in Holland, at Leiden, then had sailed to the New World as the first New England colonists. Ironically, the first New Netherland colonists also were religious refugees who had been living in Leiden at the same time. These were French Walloons, Calvinists who had fled to Holland to escape religious persecution and then had come to America to work for the Company. Leiden had been the nursery for both the English and Dutch colonies of northeastern America, once friends and fellow-travelers in the wilderness who had planted colonies, built and struggled and fought, often at each other's sides; but times had changed, and now they were at dagger points.

There was one bitter irony to console Stuyvesant as he contemplated the destruction of all he had worked for in these difficult and lonely years as director-general: the Connecticut Jankes and Governor Winthrop would also lose by the coming of the English fleet. The ships and soldiers that had just come over the ocean belonged to James Stuart, Duke of York, brother of King Charles. York was known to despise the Dutch West India Company for all the times its warships had pillaged his African colonies and merchant ships, but he loathed the Puritans of New England even more.

These English royalists were hostile to Puritan and Dutchman alike. Intending to strike at blow at the Dutch West India Company by snatching away New Netherland, the fleet also had been sent to America to intimidate the anti-royalist New Englanders. King Charles had granted all New Netherland to his brother, James — if he could take it by force. That meant the Connecticut Jankes would lose control of their coveted Long Island, which would infuriate them. Their joy at the long-awaited overthrow of Stuyvesant and New Netherland would be drained dry by being blocked in their expansionist ambitions by the Duke of York, whose most faithful commander, Sir Richard Nicolls, led this invasion fleet. Yet the New Englanders had no choice but to support Nicolls lest they be accused of treason and of challenging the rule of the royal house. At least the Jankes would be glad to put an end to New Netherland at last, and then they would take their chances with the order of things to follow.

Now, Nicolls and the fleet were at Stuyvesant's threshold, and the Long Island Jankes were already massing near the Breuckelen ferry crossing, ready to tear the city apart. Would the New Amsterdam burghers fight? There had been grumbling down in the streets that the people would have more civil rights under the Duke of York than they had as subjects of the autocratic Company, which for forty years had ruled New Netherland so clumsily, not even allowing the colonists the same rights as Dutch citizens at home. Jankes were free men who elected their own leaders, choosing the best they could, while New Netherland had their leaders forced upon them by the Company. Also, New Englanders kept the profits of their labors rather than being required to send it to mercantile lords overseas the way the New Netherlanders were compelled to do.

By now, the New Englanders virtually had independent Puritan republics, and their steadily growing strength was one reason King Charles was maneuvering to control them. The king had to be careful, however, for in the English Civil War of 1642-51 the Puritans had defeated and executed his royal father. The self-sufficient New England Puritans were far more a danger to the crown than the Dutch West India Company, which could do nothing to protect New Amsterdam. The Company had withered years ago, having lost most of its important colonies to the English, Spanish, and Portuguese. The Company had given Stuyvesant so little to work with — not enough gunpowder, too few fighting men, and a fort and city wall that were falling apart because there were no funds to maintain them. If New Amsterdam could not be held by negotiation and alliances, then the Company would not waste its money by fortifying and garrisoning it against an English and New England enemy that could easily take it.

For seventeen years, Stuyvesant's dictatorship had been the real law here, not the inconsistent admonishments of a distant, profit-hungry Company that had never profited enough from the colony. So, too, would it be today, when he led New Amsterdam in a desperate fight for its life. New Netherland was quite on its own in the world and surrounded by enemies, some of whom would destroy it more readily than show it mercy. As he stood on the tumbledown rampart of Fort Amsterdam, Director-general Pieter Stuyvesant could look over his town, the heart of New Netherland, a heart that beat only weakly. Some few volunteer militia and soldiers drilled together in the streets, but there was little martial spirit among the worried shopkeepers, traders, merchants, and craftsmen of the town, who now collected in huddled groups along the canal and in front of city hall, the *stadhuis.*

Stuyvesant had been told bluntly by his council that the people of the city wanted to make terms with the English rather than risk a disastrous battle that would end in utter destruction. The mercenary soldiers were willing enough to fight, but without the volunteer militia also rallying, there was no way the long defensive line of wall and harbor could be held against professional English soldiers and hundreds of Janke militiamen. As Stuyvesant paced the Battery, where sweating artillerymen cleaned guns, carried cannonballs and powder kegs, readied flints and matches, most of the New Amsterdammers looked on and prayed it would not come to a fight. In fact, many people would willingly transfer their allegiance to an English duke rather than live under the whim of the decaying Dutch West India Company and its strong-willed director-general. No one wanted English cannonballs crashing into their city, but more than anything else, they feared the armed Jankes gathered at the Breuckelen ferry.

Stuyvesant surveyed New Amsterdam's three hundred houses of stone and wood, most with good red tile roofs, almost all the houses with bountiful garden plots behind. Towering above the town was the double-peaked roof of the Dutch Reformed Church of St. Nicholas. To the east, beyond the streets and houses, lay a lovely expanse of green fields and groves of shady trees, where stood a small chapel that Stuyvesant himself had paid to have built. The chapel, fields, and trees were all on his personal estate, his *Bouwerij*, or farm, a place he loved, and in which folk were welcome to stroll and picnic whenever they wished.

Stuyvesant's Bouwerij and all he and the burghers had built might well be lost in the coming battle. He had sent a formal embassy to ask Nicolls why he had come to New Amsterdam, and the colonel's reply, with terms of surrender, had been to the point: "In his Majestie's Name I do demand the Town, Scituate upon the Island commonly known by the Name of Manhatoes with all the forts thereunto belonging." Stuyvesant had written a reply asserting Dutch rights to New Netherland, but Nicolls had not bothered to answer. Instead, Stuyvesant's embassy had been told that in forty-eight hours the English ships would sail into the Narrows and approach New Amsterdam. Nicolls offered magnanimous surrender terms, allowing the people to live their lives undisturbed as subjects of King Charles and residents of the proprietary colony owned by the Duke of York. The burghers soon learned about these terms, but when they insisted Stuyvesant accept them, he said he would not surrender.

Now, standing on the Battery, with the forty-eight hours drawing to a close, Stuyvesant saw two English ships sail into the North River and begin to pass slowly within range of his guns. The cannon ports of the English ships opened, and gun barrels ran out, aimed not at Fort Amsterdam, but at the defenseless city. The rest of the English fleet was anchored below Manhattan Island, royal pennons flying, their own gun-ports opened and their iron run out, ready to attack. Stuyvesant ordered his cannoneers to load and prepare to fire. The soldiers at the wall and on the fort's ramparts looked to their weapons, but the people gathered down in Broad Street were horrified, and they clamored that Stuyvesant must not do this.

The English ships came closer, the moment to fire on them almost at hand. If Stuyvesant let them pass, the ships would be in a perfect position from which to blast the town apart. He had to turn them back now, though it meant the battle would be joined. The soldier in him knew this was the decisive moment. Then Johannes Megapolensis, an elderly Dutch Reformed min-

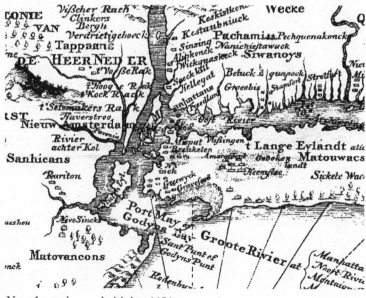

New Amsterdam and vicinity, 1656.

ister, clambered up the rampart to stand at Stuyvesant's side and cautiously ask that he not give the command to fire. The *dominee* had been in service to New Netherland even longer than Stuyvesant and had come to love the place just as much as did the director-general. He reminded Stuyvesant of the favorable terms offered by Nicolls, that the residents could keep their private property, could continue undisturbed with their businesses and their lives.

The alternative, Megapolensis warned, was death and destruction, for he had heard the ships had direct orders that "if any resistance were offered, to fire a full broadside into this open place, and so to take the city by force, and give up everything to plunder and a blood-bath." Stuyvesant said he would rather be carried out than surrender. It was hopeless, the dominee told him. Stuyvesant was fully prepared to die. Megapolensis said the people were not.

The English vessels were there now, sailing by just off the Battery, and Stuyvesant's guns were aimed, his cannoneers with lighted matches awaiting the command to fire, to begin it. Megapolensis spoke again. In God's name, what use was it to resist? Stuyvesant quivered from his fierce inner struggle. Surrendering without a fight was absolutely against his sense of duty as a soldier, for New Amsterdam was his sworn responsibility, his home, and he had done everything he could all these years for its welfare — Megapolensis lightly touched his arm. To sacrifice lives in a lost cause was not the way of a soldier…but of a madman. This was the moment to fire, guns aimed at guns, and the minister's hand pressed the director-general's arm, holding it more firmly until the moment passed.

Then Megapolensis gently drew Stuyvesant back from the rampart wall and led him away. The cannon remained silent, and the English warships sailed on to anchor triumphantly in Hudson's River.

The end of New Netherland had come, except for one final official act by Stuyvesant. In his hands were not only the surrender terms of Colonel Nicolls, but also a letter from Connecticut's Governor Winthrop, which invited any New Netherlanders who could not accept the royalist rule of the Duke of York to come and settle in Connecticut, where they would be warmly welcome. Stuyvesant tore Winthrop's letter to shreds and threw it on the floor. He wanted nothing to do with Winthrop or his colony.

If Pieter Stuyvesant could not honorably die in battle, then he would rather be a New Yorker for the rest of his life than a Connecticut Janke.

Two

YORKERS AND JANKES

If the Dutch... actually do use Jancke *(pronounced Yankee) in the sense of little John or Johnnie, then this would be the most plausible derivation, and 'Yankee Doodle' would be 'Johnnie Doodle.'*

Oscar G. Sonneck on the origin of "Yankee Doodle."

I T WAS BITTERLY COLD AT THE STOCKADED VILLAGE of Schenectady on the night of February 8, 1690, but the folk were warmed by a cheerful party celebrating the coming engagement of the minister, Peter Tassemacher. The aging Dutch Reformed dominee was soon to marry a handsome widow, who would look after him while he shepherded the little community that was known here in the northwest corner of the royal province of New York as the *"Dorp"* — the "Village."

In 1661, Schenectady had been defiantly planted on the

banks of the Mohawk as far as possible from the grasping reach of the Dutch West India Company, and later of the English governor in New York City. Now, forty good houses stood on two cross streets inside an oblong-shaped stockade that overlooked the river flats, fields, and meadows. Tassemacher's *kerk* stood near the south gate, which opened on the road to Iroquois country; the other gate, in the northeast wall, faced Albany, about twenty miles away.

Of course there was some risk to settling out here, so far from authority but also far from protection. There was again war in Europe between England and France, and it was rumored that French Canada had requisitioned fifteen hundred snowshoes to carry fighting men out on winter raids. Still, the Dorp felt secure tonight, because the weather was especially brutal and danger-ous, the more than two hundred frozen miles to Montreal virtu-ally impassable in this cold. The weather was fit only for the two comical snowmen someone had made to stand sentry at the open village gate that faced the country of the Mohawks.

One of the Five Nations of the Iroquois, the Mohawks were close allies of the English colonies. Thirty of them had come to the stockade to honor Dominee Tassemacher this evening, and with the gate open they could come and go as they pleased. The minister was much loved in this farming community just west of Albany and east of the Iroquois longhouses. He had traveled widely before settling down in 1684 as Schenectady's first man of the cloth, having served the church in the Netherlands, in South America, and in southern New

Netherland. Now he preached on the edge of the wilderness to independent-minded people who had established themselves outside the boundaries of the Van Rensselaer *patroon*, a vast land grant on both sides of Hudson's River, skirting the city of Albany and reaching all the way to the Mohawk Valley near Schenectady. Farmers who lived on the patroon were tenants, paying rent to the Van Rensselaer family — known as patroons, or lords of the manor — and the future held no promise of land ownership for a tenant.

Albany was a prosperous town of more than fifteen hundred people and was run by wealthy, politically connected fur merchants and traders who cooperated with the patroons and manorial lords of the Hudson Valley. In contrast, Schenectady was the center of a farming community of fewer than four hundred, but unlike the tenants of the patroons or the employees of the merchant class, folk here owned their homes and did as they liked with what they produced. The Dorp was beholden to no one, not to Albany merchants or patroons.

A threat from New France had arisen last fall after the warlike Iroquois had massacred two French villages near Montreal. The French wanted revenge, and it was known they believed the English colonies were behind the attacks, but what did that mean here at Schenectady, where folk had done nothing other than occasionally selling a few muskets and some powder to the Iroquois? That trade had gone on harmlessly for generations. The main stock of firearms that reached the Iroquois came from their trade with Albany, so the Village had no reason to expect

The official seal of colonial New York in the 1690s.

any trouble. There was further reason to feel secure tonight, for there were extra fighting men in the stockade, thanks to Connecticut.

Albany and Schenectady were all that stood in the way of a possible French invasion from the north, and the Albany merchants had asked New England for troops to help guard the frontier. Only Connecticut had responded, however, sending eighty men to the region. Half a dozen, under Lieutenant Enos Talmage, had recently arrived to garrison the Schenectady blockhouse. They were hearty youths, these Jankes, adventurous and brave. Many of them had volunteered to come out here because they wanted to take a close look at the northwestern frontier. The Schenectady folk had what so many Jankes hungered for: the freedom to live as they chose, on good land far from oppressive authority, whether of church or government.

Connecticut had been disappointed that the former New Netherland had not been opened up to settlement after the English takeover. Instead, royal governors had given huge land grants to their friends, and those grants had become great English-style feudal manors with their own tenant farmers, much like the Dutch patroonships. A large portion of the bountiful Hudson Valley had been shut off to the restless Jankes, unless a man wanted to serve some country lord and never aspire to building something for his children to enjoy. Now, so far from home, these young men from Connecticut were taking the opportunity to study this country with the thought of one day migrating here.

The Jankes stationed at the Dorp spoke little Dutch, and the Schenectady people spoke less English, but there was understanding enough between them. Unlike the New Netherland colonists in the south, Schenectady had never experienced much trouble with Jankes and had no cause to make up mocking verses about them to the tune of the old "Doodle-doo" song, as some called it. No doubt in some cozy bedrooms in the Village little children were being sung to sleep by older sisters or black servant aunties who knew lots of their own verses to the "Doodle-doo" tune, but Jankes were unlikely to be called doodles in them.

Actually, the tune was well known to Connecticut people, too, for their ancestors in old England had sung its nonsense rhymes to please children. Something like:

> *Lucy Locket lost her pocket,*
> *Kitty Fisher found it.*
> *Nothing in it, nothing in it,*
> *Just the binding 'round it.*

Perhaps those ancestors once had been Lowlanders themselves, for at the end of the last century more than 100,000 Flemish refugees had fled to England to escape religious persecution. They were Protestants, many of them in the cloth trade, and after a few generations of settlement in eastern England most Anglicized their names. It was in large part from these people that the Puritans drew their strength, and they had emigrated by the thousands to New England. Thus it was that the stock of the New England and New York colonizers shared a broad and deep strain of Lowland blood and heritage.

The New England Jankes had their own insults playing on versions of the Dutch name for "Johnny": one being *Jantje*, pronounced "Yan-tche," was Holland's nickname for its sailors, but to the English the term Jantje meant a pirate, which is understandable since these two sea powers had battled each other for decades. And the English liked to twist the Dutch name Jan Kees, pronounced "Yan Case" and short for Jan Cornelius, into "John Cheese" — the Dutch being known for their favorite food.

On this winter's night the potential threat from New France and any old suspicions between New Yorker and New Englander were set aside for the sake of good Dominee Tassemacher's engagement celebration. Most of the folk inside the stockade shared in the fun, eating, drinking, and singing. As the children of the Dorp nodded off, their elders feasted around tables laden with abundant, delicious food and drink — a sight that was a marvel to the Connecticut Jankes. At home in the depth of winter, their folk ate sparingly of what had been hoarded from a harvest that was only grudgingly yielded by their stony land. There was so much to be learned from the innovative Dutch — not to mention how to fulfill the dream that many a bold young militiaman had of journeying into the forest like a Dutch *bosloper*, a "forest runner," who traded with wild savages for a fortune in furs.

These young soldiers wanted to know more about Dutch

methods of farming and animal husbandry, and how they created their fine homesteads. The Dutch in the colonies were progressive builders, using finished lumber and shingles turned out by water-powered sawmills instead of being limited to the rough hand-sawn boards, hewn logs, and thatch roofs that were so common elsewhere. Colonial Dutch homes were adorned with beautiful imported furniture from Holland, elegant but practical housewares and crockery, and decorative tiles; they were served by marvelously effective brick ovens and lit by plenty of windows, always at least one of which had stained glass. New Englanders were fast learning to copy Dutch styles and inventions — farming tools and systems, sleighs, skates, sawmills, brick-making, hothouses....

In New England, when something was cleverly devised or improved upon, the popular saying was that it "beat the Dutch."

Using farming methods and implements that were highly regarded in both Europe and America, Dutch settlers had made the most of the rich soil and dense forests of the Mohawk River Valley. Dutch skill in animal husbandry, garden vegetables, and fruit-growing had made them the envy of those who tried to imitate them. The Indian peoples, too, had been quick to adopt their fruits and vegetables, which by now were grown throughout the wilderness wherever Dutch traders made an appearance with goods that included seeds as well as tools.

Though impressed by the Dutch, the Connecticut militia company had brought along a reputation of its own: for Indian-fighting. Back in the 1670s New Englanders had decisively defeated their region's most powerful tribes in a prolonged, desperate war. Here on the New York frontier, however, there had been little conflict between the white colonists and their Indian neighbors. No one could deny that things were changing, however, and that troubles were looming with the French and their Algonquin allies.

Still, on this winter night in 1690 few people thought any troops would be needed around Schenectady until springtime, when French and Indian raiding parties might be abroad. It was generally assumed the raiders would be looking for Iroquois villages, not white towns, to wipe out in revenge for the recent massacres. So far, the American colonies of England and France had an unspoken agreement to avoid taking part in the recurring wars that hurled their home countries at each other's throats. Wars stopped commerce, brought ruin upon the colonies, and in this region just the threat of fighting wrenched the fur trade to a sudden halt.

When the Iroquois or French were on the warpath against each other, the northern woods became fraught with danger, every route of travel offering sites for ambush, every village and trading post vulnerable to raids. Whether danger was imminent or not in northern New York this winter, most people were glad to have the Connecticut troops in the region. There were others, however, particularly in Schenectady, who had objections. It was not personal animosity behind the hard feelings some had for the Connecticut troops. Instead, it was caused by tumultuous colonial politics and festering civil conflict that had painfully divided the people of New York. Schenectady supported one side of the dispute, Albany the other, and the Janken soldiers were caught in the middle.

There had been frequent periods of turmoil since 1664, when the English first took New Netherland. (The Dutch had recaptured New York City in 1673 only to return it a year later by the terms of a peace treaty.) Now there was even more turmoil, for in 1688 King James II had been driven from the English throne, and his regime's colonial governors in New England and New York had been thrown out.

A New York City faction made up mainly of older Dutch colonists and some English Long Islanders had taken control of the colonial government. They declared that they would give up power only when King William and Queen Mary, successors to James, sent over a new governor. Because this upstart faction opposed commercial monopolies and intended to break them, Albany's rich merchants feared losing the lucrative fur-trade prerogatives they had been granted by the royal governor. Albany merchants were so set against the New York City faction that they accused its leaders of treason and rebellion. On the other hand, most people in Schenectady backed the faction because they wanted to be free to enter the fur trade. To supplement their farming and lumbering enterprises, the settlers here had always carried on a little illegal bartering with the Indians. Since the Village was closer than Albany to the longhouses, it was infuriating to be forbidden by law to develop a real trading post. The political power had always belonged to the Albany merchant clique, however, so when they complained about illegal fur trading, the people of Schenectady were brought to heel.

With the fall of King James, times were changing and apparently turning against the wealthy colonial establishment, which included both Dutch and English. Until now, that establishment had held monopolies embracing every aspect of colonial business: the fur trade, shipping, fishing, whaling, flour-milling, bread-making, barrel-making, exporting, port privileges, the carrying trades, and brewing. Everyone else was closed out from entering these livelihoods unless they cooperated with the monopolists. Such oppressive economic conditions did not exist in England or Holland, but they dominated life in New York. These days, the Schenectady Dutch and Long Island English found themselves allied against the establishment because the Long Islanders also loathed the monopolies. For one thing, they wanted to trade directly with New England, which until now they could do only by smuggling.

To some folk in Schenectady, the Connecticut troops were no more than the hired mercenaries of the Albany merchants who had requested them, and there was concern that the Jankes might one day be used as an occupation force that would stifle future support of the New York City faction. To make matters worse, the faction had come up and nominated its own set of officials to govern Schenectady, and that had caused arguments over who should be in command of whatever soldiers were in the Village. Although Dominee Tassenmacher's happiness had brought many of the villagers together tonight, the folk were so divided that violence had been threatened if one side or the other tried to take control of the troops.

Disgruntlement ran so deep that when Peter Schuyler, Albany's mayor, warned the Dorp three days ago to prepare to defend against French and Indian raiders, he was told to mind his own business. Schenectady had always managed its Indian affairs, and had done it well. The proof lay in the fact that although wars with the tribes had broken out elsewhere, this region had remained quiet. Because of the feud, the Connecticut men were not even allowed to post sentries in the stockade. Of course, no Janken or Schenectady militiaman relished tramping back and forth along an icy rampart on such a harsh night. It even seemed about to snow.

By eleven o'clock the celebration had ended, and everyone made their way homeward to fall deep asleep behind barred doors. Lieutenant Talmage was quartered with the Sweer Teunise family, his soldiers in their blockhouse. While Schenectady Dutch and Connecticut Jankes slept contentedly that winter's night, only the snowmen stood watch at the stockade's south gate, which was still open.

At midnight, in the depth of darkness, two shadows flitted past the snowmen by the gate. One shadow went to the right, the other to the left. More shadows quickly followed, swift and sure, as silent as the snowmen, so that not even a dog was aroused. Within moments each shadow took its place until the houses and blockhouse of the Dorp were surrounded, every one, and still there was silence.

When the first two shadows had gone all the way along the stockade walls and met each other at the far end of the sleeping village, the time had come. A war shriek rang out, a wail of death instantly joined by two hundred other howling voices, and muskets banged, axes thudded against splintering doors, windows were forced open. Screeches of battle-madness echoed with screams of terror and agony and with the roars of men who had been caught unarmed. Flames burst from open windows, victims were dragged out of doors to be tomahawked in the street. Mothers had children torn away and saw them savagely killed. Schenectady had no chance.

The blockhouse door was battered down and in rushed a swarm of French and Indians. The Connecticut soldiers fought gallantly but without hope. Talmage, their lieutenant, defended the Teunise house along with four black slaves, but the enemy broke in and put them all to the sword, including Sweer Teunise and two womenfolk. The house was torched, and one after the other the buildings of the Village went up in flames.

For two hours the fighting and screaming and murdering went on, from house to house, bedroom to cellar, in back alleys and out in the streets, until at last the bloodlust of the attackers was sated. Then began the age-old custom of chivalrously granting mercy after the slaughter was done. Prisoners were rounded up and huddled together under guard. Some people had escaped, but sixty were dead — thirty-eight men and boys, the rest being women and children. Dominee Tassemacher, like many of his neighbors, lay dead in his burning home. Twenty-seven males were taken prisoner to be marched back as trophies to Montreal, if they survived the ordeal. They were mostly boys, although three Connecticut soldiers were among them.

The thirty visiting Mohawks were spared because of the lasting affection of the attacking warriors, who were known as "Praying Indians." They, too, were Mohawks, but they had been converted to Catholicism by French Jesuit priests and had left the valley to live near Montreal. The Praying Indians had been assured that an attack on Schenectady would not harm their Mohawk kinfolk.

Before morning, it began to snow.

England and France had been at war for more than a year, but until now their American colonies had avoided being dragged into the conflict.

It was the fur trade with the Indians that had brought both the first Dutch and French adventurers to this part of the New World, and at the start there had been plenty for all. Lately, however, the powerful Iroquois had grabbed for a fur monopoly of their own. They had attacked other tribes and nations, mostly Algonquins, trying to force them to sell their furs only to the Iroquois, who traded exclusively with Albany. This meant New France was losing its fur commerce, so it joined the Algonquins to fight the Iroquois in a bloody back-and-forth conflict that had turned dramatically against the French. Last autumn's dis-

In the winter of 1690, French and Mohawk raiders from New France massacred the Dutch settlement at Schenectady in New York Province.

astrous assaults by the Iroquois had destroyed French villages on the very doorstep of Montreal, with more than two hundred men, women, and children slain, and many carried off never to come home again.

As far as the government of New France was concerned, the whites around Albany and Schenectady had French blood on their hands because of selling firearms to the Iroquois. The French believed these "English" of northern New York had encouraged the Iroquois to extend their fur-acquiring empire for the benefit of Albany and at the expense of Montreal. New France was desperate for a victory, its future clouded by the triumphs of the Iroquois. The Algonquins were wavering in their loyalty, afraid they would be the next to feel the weight of an Iroquois attack. New France had to prove it was not defeated, and also had to awe the Iroquois, who might still be brought to a peace conference. The Algonquins were reluctant to join in raids against the English, but there were the "Praying Indians," who would willingly follow Jesuit priests into battle.

Furthermore, Louis XIV of France had demanded his colonial subjects strike a decisive blow against the British in North America. After being deposed, England's King James had fled to the protection of Louis, his friend and fellow Catholic, and that had brought on another war between England and France. The Protestant rulers of the Netherlands, Prince William of Orange and his consort, Mary, daughter of James, had ascended to the English throne. In William, Louis faced one of his most formidable foes, a brilliant and determined tactician who once had

looded the Dutch fields to stop Louis's advancing armies from
capturing Amsterdam. Then the Dutch had decisively defeated
the French at sea, foiling Louis's plans for final conquest of the
Low Countries. Now, Louis demanded a victory over the
English in America, thus to humiliate William.

New France did not have much of a regular army, but it did
have tough forest fighters, daring soldiers of fortune and fur
traders who could strike at Albany, even in winter. The French
reckoned that once the English had been severely punished, they
would no longer support the Iroquois, who would find themselves alone against New France and her own Indian allies. The
destruction of Schenectady was the opening of a new and bloody
era of conflict in North America. For much of the next seventy
years the British and French colonies would make savage war
with each other and with their allied Indian nations.

The Albany Dutch and their Mohawk friends organized
hot pursuit of the enemy raiders who had massacred
Schenectady. In the vicinity of Montreal they caught and
killed twenty-five stragglers who had slowed down because they
thought they were safely home. This was the first invasion of
Canada by the English colonies, and it would be followed by others, a succession of clumsy failures that left New Englanders and
New Yorkers embittered about the blood and money wasted
against New France.

The first attempt was late in 1690, when a fleet of thirty-four
colonial ships and two thousand militia and sailors went up the

Saint Lawrence to attack Quebec. Also, an army moved down Lake Champlain to join the campaign, but inexperience, hardship, and dissension caused this wing of the invasion to give up before it ever reached Canada. Just in time, the French managed to organize a defense against the fleet, which withdrew, beaten and dispirited.

Between interludes of peace, new wars erupted again and again between England and France — King William's War was eight years; Queen Anne's War, eleven; King George's War was four. With few regular British soldiers in the colonies, the burden was borne by militiamen and their amateur officers, and by the sailors in privateers that cruised the coastline of Maine and Acadia, hunting for French prizes in the very mouth of the Saint Lawrence. Support from England was negligible, and New France repelled each invasion while its raiders destroyed frontier communities in

New York and New England almost at will. Year after year people were barbarously slaughtered in the settlements, thousands of frightened folk abandoning their hard-won homes to escape the raiders. Even villages nestled in the heart of Massachusetts were stricken by French and Indian fighters, who carried out superhuman feats of endurance as they hurried through winter forests to surprise the settlements.

A lasting hatred for the French and their Indians came over the war-weary people of English America, yet they were determined to succeed one day in a decisive invasion of Canada. They tried again in 1707, when a colonial fleet and militia troops joined fifteen British ships of war, six store ships, and seven thousand regulars on forty transports — all under a full admiral. The most powerful expedition ever assembled in America, it sailed into the Gulf of Saint Lawrence aiming to attack Quebec town. Incompetent leadership

Surviving settlers flee through the snow as French and Indian attackers burn Schenectady in February of 1690, during one of the first frontier conflicts to erupt between New France and British America.

ran the fleet onto the rocks of the Saint Lawrence River's north shore, and eight vessels went down, drowning a thousand men. This attempt, too, was abandoned in grief and sorrow and in shame.

After Queen Anne's War ended by treaty in 1713, there was peace for thirty-one years, but frustration and smoldering anger pervaded New England and New York. Meanwhile, New France grew stronger as fortifications were built, most notably Fortress Louisbourg on the Atlantic coast, which took twenty-five years to construct and was considered one of the great bastions in the world. Further strengthening New France were regiments of regular troops who were shipped over from Europe. Most of these soldiers would never return home again, for when they left the military they were expected to become settlers and members of a local militia company.

In these years the English colonies prospered, their populations increasing swiftly, but the general opinion was that their frontiers would remain a no-man's land, with no room to expand until New France was finally defeated. In 1744, King George's War broke out over the dispute about who should be the next ruler of Austria, and the New Englanders decided it was time to move against New France once again. Undaunted after generations of failure, they were determined to attack the most impregnable objective of all, Fortress Louisbourg. Since crown and Parliament could not afford to send another army to the colonies, they expected to do it without the aid of British regulars or generals.

The military experts declared it suicidal, saying militiamen would never serve in a long campaign while fields at home wanted tending, nor would they garrison winter outposts far from family and hearth. Professional regulars were needed — king's redcoats and experienced commanders with their commissary staffs, supply and ordnance officers, artillerymen, and mapmakers. No homespun gaggle of militia yokels could stand up to the French regulars and their forest fighters.

At this time, the only permanent military establishment in the British colonies was made up of the few hundred men in four ill-disciplined, poorly trained Independent Companies that had been raised in Britain and were headquartered in New York. Though considered regulars, these soldiers were useless for anything other than garrison duty. Many of their men and officers were on the outlook for the main chance to profit from colonial opportunities such as land speculation. One of them was military surgeon Richard Shuckburgh, an ambitious Englishman who had come to New York in the 1730s.

By 1744, the thirty-four-year-old Dr. Shuckburgh was well connected in New York City society and associated with men who were bent on cornering the land market in the Mohawk Valley. All that stood between them and their fortunes was New France and its Indian allies — although no one denied these were formidable obstacles, indeed.

Three

SONG OF INSULT

Brother Ephraim sold his cow
To buy him a commission,
And then he went to Canada
To fight for the nation.

When his commission he had got,
He proved an arrant coward,
He dared not go to Cape Breton
For fear he'd be devoured.

Pre-Revolution verses of "Yankee Doodle."

A GENTLEMAN OF INFINITE JEST AND HUMOR," they said of Dr. Richard Shuckburgh, surgeon to the redcoats of the Four Independent Companies. They sometimes added that Dr. Shuckburgh preferred drinking to doctoring.

Yet, by the spring of 1745 it was widely acknowledged that Shuckburgh, who was stationed in Albany, knew more about the Five Nations of the Iroquois than any colonist save for his friend and mentor, William Johnson. An Irish-born adventurer, about the same age as Shuckburgh, Johnson lived in the Mohawk Valley, forty miles west of Albany. He was considered a chieftain among the Mohawks, an adopted son, and he had fought alongside them, traded with them, smoked with them, and had fathered a number of children with their women. Johnson had greater influence with the Five Nations than did any other white man.

A close Johnson ally, Shuckburgh was a commissioned redcoat officer, but he was also involved in land speculation, collaborating with prominent New Yorkers — some of them also friends and associates of Johnson's — all seeking to purchase Indian lands along the Mohawk and Delaware rivers. One day the migrations from New England would burst past the patroons and manors of New York, and then land-hungry pioneers would be prime customers for the men who held title to the country west of Albany and Schenectady. No one could persuade the Iroquois to sell land the way William Johnson could persuade them; he was not only well connected to chiefs of the Iroquois, but also to important men in New York colony.

Johnson's uncle and patron was Commodore Peter Warren, a dashing Englishman who had married an heiress of the powerful De Lancey family of New York City. A resident of the city when he was not at sea cruising after privateers and pirates — and Frenchmen if there was a war on at the time — Warren also served on the provincial council. He had acquired title to thousands of acres of land in the Mohawk Valley, then sent Johnson there to represent him in matters of Indian trade, building outposts, and purchasing more land. Johnson had outdone himself, taking to the life of frontier merchant and land speculator with enthusiasm, acuteness, and courage, bringing both Warren and himself great financial reward. In winning Iroquois trade Johnson had even outmaneuvered most of the longtime Albany Dutch merchants.

Men like Richard Shuckburgh were ideal allies to Johnson and Warren. For one thing, the colonial government based in New York City wanted Englishmen in positions of influence on the Albany-Mohawk frontier, men who could undercut the tight-knit society of the Dutchmen, most of whom spoke English only as a second language. Sometimes the governor even sent a New Englander to run some important colonial office in the Albany region, knowing that "Yankees" still had a natural-born hostility to the upper Hudson Valley Dutch. (These days, English-speaking New Yorkers often referred to New Englanders with their own pronunciation of "Jankes" — "Yankees.")

Beyond practicing medicine among the soldiers, civilians, and Indians, Shuckburgh worked with Johnson to plan for the future sale of lands. Already, the New Englanders wanted room to settle down and farm property of their own, and thousands were moving into the Hudson Valley, some legally, others illegally. The definite borders between Connecticut and New York were still being argued over, and many Yankees were squatters on land claimed by a manor or patroon. Even those who had bought lands directly from Indians, as many had done from the Wappingers in New York's Dutchess County, might find their titles challenged. They were doomed one day to be thrown off or forced to become tenants. Many would be moving on, and the Mohawk Valley and beyond would eventually open up to settlement.

William Johnson, adopted son of the Mohawks, held the key to this country. His ally Shuckburgh had spent the past ten years in the Mohawk Valley, even longer than Johnson, who had arrived in 1737. Shuckburgh had been out surveying lands in 1735, and in 1736 had been at the government trading post at Oswego on Lake Ontario, where he had furnished medicine for militia and Iroquois. As an officer in the regular army, he had attended colonial conferences with the tribes, and he was attentive to the unfolding developments between the colonial government and the fiercely independent Iroquois.

Most of the Albany and Hudson Valley Dutch were hostile to William Johnson, their toughest competitor in the Indian trade, but Shuckburgh was on good terms with the burghers and patroons. Born into a landed family of Warwickshire gentry in

England, he easily adapted to the most refined of colonial company. He was welcomed by the best Dutch families, including the Van Rensselaers, who invited him to Fort Crailo, the family manor house in Green Bush on the east side of Hudson's River, across from Albany.

The original house on the site of this handsome brick mansion had been built in 1642. The minister Johannes Megapolensis, he who had persuaded Pieter Stuyvesant not to fire on the English, had lived there while serving the Rensselaerwyck patroon. The dominee arrived from Holland the same year as the original house was built, and his name was inscribed on a foundation stone still visible in the cellar. The later house had been enlarged over the years, loopholed for muskets, and able to withstand Indian attack. The Dutch name of the house was after an estate of the Van Rensselaers in Holland, called Crailo, and meaning "Crows' Wood."

Not only was Richard Shuckburgh well liked here in the Hudson Valley, but he also had prominence in New York City because he was the husband of the former Mary Gardiner, descendant of Lionel Gardiner, a Scottish military engineer who had been in the army of the Netherlands and was later an officer in the Connecticut forces. Lionel's wife had been Dutch, coming with her husband to America and helping to build the family manor on Gardiner's Island. Thus, Mary Shuckburgh had her own Dutch heritage to recommend her to the Albany folk.

While the Dutch of New York City and Long Island had merged and intermarried with the mainly English and Scottish colonists, the Dutch families of the river valleys still had things pretty much their own way. Church services were yet in the old language, so even the explosive "Great Awakening" of religious fervor and camp meetings that was sweeping New England had little effect in rural New York. The Dutch here were content with their own religion, which was the center of their community, and they did not need English-speaking evangelists to raise a hullabaloo about the state of their souls. The old Dutch families well knew who they were, and therefore the hysterical

The Van Rensselaer mansion in Green Bush (now Rensselaer), called Fort Crailo, circa 1790; the back wing was added after the 1755 muster of British and colonial troops during the French and Indian wars.

sermons of Yankee Bible-thumpers held little interest for them.

Some of the Dutch Reformed congregations in and around New York City were dropping the old customs and language, and a few were converting to become Presbyterian or even Anglican. Their young folk were learning English more readily than Dutch, which seemed backward and old-fashioned to the new generation in the city. If a man wanted to advance in English society there, it was advisable not to boast about having Dutch blood. To the upcountry folk, New York City Dutchmen were not that far from being Englishmen.

Much about Dr. Richard Shuckburgh appealed to both the English and Dutch of the province. He was charming socially, jovial and full of fun, a ready wit and a hearty companion. In business matters he was an excellent clerk who could record meetings and transactions and handle correspondence, whether for the army or business associates or for Johnson. Shuckburgh's skills as a doctor might have been largely self-taught, but he was regarded favorably by Dr. Alexander Hamilton, a Scottish-born physician from Maryland who was touring the Northeast in 1744. The formally educated Hamilton met Shuckburgh during a visit to Fort Crailo, when they dined with the patroon, Johannes van Rensselaer.

Calling the Englishman "Shakesburrough," Hamilton later wrote that "by his conversation [he] seemed to have as little of the quack in him as any half-hewn doctor ever I had met with. The doctors of Albany are mostly Dutch, all empirics, having no knowledge or learning but what they have acquired by bare experience. They study chiefly the virtues of herbs, and the woods here furnish their shops with all the pharmacy they use."

Like his business associates, friends, and neighbors, Shuckburgh hoped for a lasting peace in the north country of New York colony, but this was not to be. Darkening the horizon of Shuckburgh's and Johnson's enterprises was yet another war between England and France. Yorkers on the frontier hoped at first to keep out of it, but then came the troubling news that the New England colonies had united for an all-out assault on Fortress Louisbourg on Cape Breton. The over-confident Yankees resolved to attack the fortress because it harbored privateers that threatened shipping, and it competed with New England's commercial fishermen by offering French fishing fleets a convenient haven.

In all of America, there were no available British troops or generals to lead the expedition, so it simply had to fail. What was worse, attacking Louisbourg surely would stir up the Canadians and their Indian allies, who would launch brutal reprisals wherever they could hit hard and get away quickly. Albany and Schenectady, on the edge of the wilderness, were as vulnerable as ever to such murderous raids.

Before setting foot on craggy Cape Breton in May of 1745, most militiamen of the New England colonies hardly knew what a fortress was. By early June, they did know, as mighty gates and massive stone walls loomed above them, and French artillery thundered defiantly day after day. Still, these untrained, blissfully ignorant New Englanders had no doubt they would capture Fortress Louisbourg sometime soon.

Four thousand militia volunteers from Massachusetts, Connecticut, Rhode Island, and New Hampshire were encamped in straggling siege works on the landward sides of the fortified town. The very audacity of their first daring landing with small boats on the rocky shoreline had surprised the garrison. The New Englanders had rushed inland, and "everyone did what was right in his own eyes," as one soldier said. They immediately captured an abandoned artillery strongpoint that provided the much-needed heavy guns to bombard the fortress. More New England batteries were put in place, but only after the grueling labors of thousands of militiamen struggling like beasts of burden to manhandle cannon from ship to shore,

SIEGE OF LOUISBOURG.
1745.

then through boggy swamps and up hillsides. Under cover of night and fog, the invaders worked themselves steadily closer to the fortress.

Teams of two or three hundred sweating men were harnessed to each heavy gun, which they hauled and pushed a yard at a time throughout the night. Shoes were lost in mud, clothing torn, limbs bruised and scraped. Near the front, in daylight, there was nowhere for exhausted men to sleep save under bushes, while French cannonballs crashed and bounced around them.

Doing what was right in their own eyes, these "Jonathans," as New Englanders often were nicknamed — sometimes "Brother Jonathan" by other colonists and also by the English — proved themselves tough and brave, willing and self-sacrificing, as they tightened the noose on Louisbourg. The campaign had all the zeal of a crusade, of a holy war against popery and Catholic

Fortress Louisbourg in May 1745, when New England militia landed west of the town and began a siege that resulted in the French surrender late in June.

France and against the hellhound Canadians and Indians who year after year cruelly murdered their people. These volunteers were fighting to defend their Protestant faith and to rid colonial frontiers of a deadly enemy. Their passion drove them to accomplish astounding feats of endurance and courage as they moved the guns ever closer, then served them under musketry and accurate cannonading laid down by the enemy's veteran artillerymen.

It did help morale that the men expected to pillage the town and return home wealthier than when they left. It also helped to have an allowance of rum each day to sustain them. More important than any other factor, however, was militia general William Pepperell, their able, if inexperienced, commander. A prosperous merchant from Kittery, Maine, General Pepperell knew from the start that his men would obey only their own officers, so it had been essential that each participating colony give him a separate commission to lead its troops. He bore a great and difficult responsibility with patience and wisdom, holding his force of four thousand individualists together and maintaining the siege against all the odds.

The cannonading went on, fortress to entrenchment and back again, and although the New Englanders battered the fortified town to bits, shuddering the fortress doors with cannonballs, the French would not surrender. Discipline and morale among the garrison's five hundred and sixty regulars and fourteen hundred militia could have been better, though, because most of the regulars had reluctantly come to Cape Breton. For a French soldier, service in North America was as good as exile, and Louisbourg was the loneliest post, remote from everywhere. No wonder there had been a brief mutiny last winter over inadequate pay and miserable living conditions. Now, after a month of siege, their quarters and the town lay blasted to shambles, with hundreds of miserable civilians trapped in the distress and horror.

Yet it was unimaginable to think that these unsoldierly *Bostonnais*, as the French called New Englanders, would be able to sustain a siege long enough to make the defenders capitulate. Such logic made sense, as hundreds of invaders fell ill because of filthy camp conditions. At the worst time of sickness almost two thousand invaders were laid low with bouts of fever and dysentery. Nevertheless, Pepperell held them together, and his men were determined to outlast the garrison.

In spite of the hardships, most New Englanders recovered from their weakness and found a way to make the best of soldiering so far from home. For all the rigors of siege warfare, whenever it was fine weather the camp behind the lines usually took on the atmosphere of a rollicking country fair. While the artillerymen banged away at each other, the off-duty militia cavorted in their grubby encampments of sailcloth tents and huts of sod, pine boughs, and bark. In the sprawling camp men were rowdy and raucous, holding contests in footracing, wrestling, boxing, pitching quoits, cudgel-fighting, and even in target-shooting with their scarce powder and lead. Their officers joined in as equals. It was also sport to chase down bouncing French cannonballs that had spent their force, and then carry them to the gunners for sending back at the enemy.

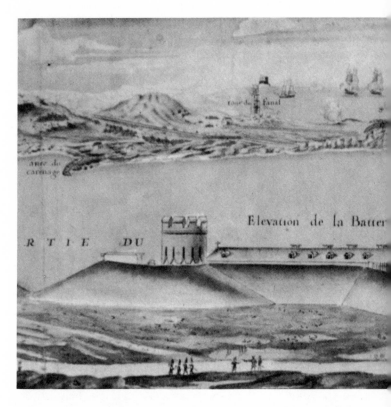

A French elevation of the Royal Battery at Fortress Louisbourg, showing the British fleet blockading the harbor and Pepperrell's militiamen hauling cannon into position; the island battery that was unsuccessfully attacked at night by the New Englanders is in the bay, right of center.

Crowds mingled, whites and blacks together, free men and bondsmen, upper classes and lower, and they delighted in mad-dash horse racing, rough hilarity, and swilling rum. There was ballad singing, fiddle playing, and fifing, to which the men danced and jigged the idle hours away. Their own version of the "Doodle-doo" tune included verses that could be sung during square dancing to call out the movements:

> *Stand up, Jonathan*
> *Figure in by neighbor,*
> *I' faith, then, stand a little off*
> *And make the room some wider.*

Other verses were about the festivities at home during town election days, when there would be lots of rum-drinking, or "lapping 'lasses," as rum was made from molasses:

> *'Lection time is now at hand,*
> *We're going to Father Chase's,*
> *There'll be some a-drinking 'round,*
> *And others lappin' 'lasses.*

Some verses were a bit racy:

> *Heigh ho for our Cape Cod,*
> *Heigh ho, Nantasket,*
> *Do not let the Boston wags*
> *Feel your oyster basket!*

Two and two may go to bed,
Two and two together,
And if there is not room enough,
Lie one atop t'other.

A favorite, but dangerous, diversion of Brother Jonathan while campaigning at Cape Breton was to tramp off whenever he had a mind to hunt or fish along the pretty streams and rocky coast, or to go after lobsters in the ocean pools. Too often, unsuspecting soldiers became the prey, hunted down by the Abenaki allies of the French. They became "fresh meat," as the warriors often called those victims who were ritually cannibalized, a common fate for prisoners of the Indians. When some men did not return to the New England camp it might be whispered that they had been taken, killed, and devoured.

On Sundays, these sons of the Puritans remembered their homes, families, and their faith as they gathered for meeting, in open-air sermons that were four-hour hellfire and brimstone exhortations to fight against those devil's tools defending the fortress. One of the most strident Sabbath day voices carrying above those thousands of homesick, somber young men was that of the Rev. Samuel Moody, the seventy-year-old senior chaplain of the expedition. A tyrannical despot over his congregation in York, Maine, Parson Moody had brought along a sharpened axe with which he intended to chop to pieces the parish church altar in Louisbourg.

When, after weeks of siege, an assault of some sort was called for, Pepperell planned a stealthy night attack against an artillery battery on the island that protected the entrance to the harbor. After midnight on June 6, four hundred and fifty men in dozens of whaleboats — equipped with paddles especially made for a silent approach — slid through the darkness toward the heavily fortified island. Despite the crashing surf, the leaders found a small landing place between the rocks, and the men began to come ashore in two or three boats at a time, all that could fit into the narrow gap between the boulders. The hushed landing went on, and soon a hundred and fifty men were ashore. They gathered under the great walls of the bastion, French sentries unaware of their presence. Scaling ladders ready, the excited attackers impatiently awaited the arrival of the remaining men from the other boats still on the water. Then some excited fool, perhaps expecting an easy victory, or who was drunk, called on his friends to give three rousing hurrahs, which erupted in the darkness.

The alarm rang out, and the French garrison awoke, springing to their cannon, swivels, and small arms. The night blazed and thundered, grapeshot and musket balls hailing down on the men on the rocky shoreline and raking across the water where the rest of the whaleboats floated helplessly. Boats were hit and splintered, many sinking with all their men, while others paddled away out of range. On shore, the troops made a desperate attempt to scale the walls, but they were beaten back to huddle among rocks, hiding from the enemy's murderous fire. At dawn, they surrendered. Nearly half the original attacking force was killed, wounded, or captured. All Pepperell could do now was intensify his artillery bombardments, moving guns even closer; after two more weeks he finally obliterated the very same island battery that had cost so many lives in the unsuccessful assault.

Time was on the side of the New Englanders, for the British Navy had arrived to cooperate with the expedition. Under Commodore Peter Warren — Mohawk Valley land speculator, nabob of colonial politics, and uncle to William Johnson — a task force off shore was capturing or driving away any French warship that tried to break through the blockade of Louisbourg. Warren was also taking enemy merchant ships as valuable prizes. It was a profitable venture, for captured prizes were later sold off, and the officers and men of Warren's squadron all shared in the money (the admiral's being by far the greatest portion). Meanwhile the New England militiamen blundering around and dying in the darkness, standing guard in muddy entrenchments far from home, eating miserable food, and sleeping in dirty hovels day after day, had no claim at all on the riches won by the fleet. Brother Jonathan fought his battle but saw not a penny of the million pounds sterling earned by Warren, half of which went to the king and half to the men of the naval squadron.

When, on June 26, the final land assault was to take place, with Warren's ships about to storm into the harbor, cannons roaring and marines landing, a flag of truce rose above the fortress, and French drums beat out the signal for a parley. The hungry, shell-shocked defenders wanted no more, and they surrendered. The keys of the city were formally handed over to Pepperell: both he and Warren would be knighted by King George II.

News of the triumph made every bell in New England ring out jubilantly, as did bells in New York, Philadelphia, and Williamsburg. There were fireworks and bonfires and days of thanksgiving as the news spread all over America and Europe that Cape Breton was taken — and taken by Americans. All the world was amazed to hear that an undisciplined, ragged colonial militia army alone could have captured famous Fortress Louisbourg. Not a few in the British military establishment were jealous of the feat, many preferring to believe a report that the French had actually surrendered to Warren, the British commodore, and not to Pepperell, the Yankee militia general. It annoyed New Englanders to hear this false report was circulating in America and Britain.

Pepperell's militiamen were stunned and furious when he gave orders not to loot the city. According to the surrender terms, the French soldiers and civilians were allowed to take all they could carry when they withdrew. This was galling to the militiamen, who had eagerly anticipated at least this reward for all their efforts. Only one of them was permitted to do as he chose, and that was Parson Moody, who vented his hatred against the Catholic church, viciously wielding his hatchet on the icons and altar, destroying the sanctuary just as the cannon had destroyed the city.

Remarkable as leading the capture of Fortress Louisbourg

was, General Pepperell's powers of persuasion were also considerable, as he convinced hundreds of disgusted militiamen to remain on Cape Breton until British regulars arrived to replace them. The wounded and ill and those whose homes were in perilous frontier locations sailed for New England, where they were greeted as returning heroes. As for the poor fellows left behind to garrison bleak and ruined Louisbourg, where scarcely a roof was still intact, they faced the onset of cold, wet, and dreary weather. Autumn passed with no force of regulars arriving to replace them as had been promised by the government in Britain, and the months dragged on.

Ice blocked the harbor and the sea road home. Grave illness came upon the men. During the campaign, they had lost only a hundred soldiers to enemy fire, but in that harsh and relentless

French soldiers drill at firing by volley on command.

winter of 1745-46, another thousand took sick and died. The ground was too frozen to bury them, so they were stacked beneath the floorboards, awaiting spring to come to that dismal, despised, storm-swept fortress. New England's triumph had been great. Its sacrifice became ever greater.

By the terms of the Aix-la-Chapelle peace treaty two years later, the British government calculated that Madras, India, was worth far more than Fortress Louisbourg, so in exchange for Madras, Louisbourg was blithely returned to the French. The New Englanders were shocked, dismayed, and deeply hurt. Never would they forgive Britain for what she had done.

Ten years after the expedition against Cape Breton, Dr. Richard Shuckburgh returned to New York City from a trip to London, where he had been managing business affairs for himself and his associates, including William Johnson. On September 2, 1755, Shuckburgh sailed into the harbor in company with Sir Charles Hardy, the new governor of the colony, a good man to know. Throughout the three-month-long voyage Shuckburgh's wit had enlivened Sir Charles's party, although they knew serious trouble awaited them in America.

France was winning the latest American war, as from the wilderness of the Ohio Valley to the shores of Lake Ontario British arms had been decisively crushed. That July the most terrible disaster had befallen a powerful force of British regulars under General Edward Braddock. Ambushed in western

Pennsylvania, the proud Braddock and more than nine hundred men had fallen, the remnants of the army escaping mainly because of the intrepid rearguard actions of Virginia provincials commanded by their colonel, George Washington. On that doomed march had been Shuckburgh's own company, commanded by Captain Horatio Gates, who had somehow survived. If fate had taken a different turn, Shuckburgh would have been with them and might have died on that bloody wilderness road instead of being on a visit to England, enjoying the theaters and delights of London.

No force of British regulars was left anywhere in America to replace the troops lost with Braddock. The frontiers were ablaze, thousands of farms and scores of settlements destroyed by rampaging French-allied Indians. Settlers had fled by the thousands to larger towns, hoping the enemy would not come there, too, and massacre them all. There was only one hope for the embattled folk on the northern frontiers, and that was a raw provincial army of three thousand men that William Johnson had led into the wilds around Lake George, fifty miles north of Albany.

Aiming to capture the French fort at Crown Point on Lake Champlain, Johnson's army was made up of New England and New York militia along with five hundred Iroquois. Awaiting them was a French and Indian army of comparable size, but under the command of a senior general who had with him two hundred crack regulars. Colonel Johnson's second-in-command was Colonel Phineas Lyman of Connecticut, who like many of his own officers and men had fought and won at Louisbourg.

Lyman knew more about campaigning than Johnson did, so there was much dissension in the army, for the New Englanders wanted Lyman in charge, and the New Yorkers and Indians wanted Johnson.

Hearing about the impending battle, Shuckburgh was anxious to join Johnson, but before he could set off upriver, the disheartening news arrived that the French and Indians had won the first engagement. Shuckburgh rushed from the city, taking the first boat he could that was sailing up Hudson's River. Governor Hardy and his staff hurried close behind, meaning to rally whatever emergency force could be mustered as a desperate second line of defense at Albany. Dread hung heavily over the Hudson Valley, whose people might at any moment hear the enemy was approaching, destroying everything in their path.

More militia troops were on the move toward Albany, including companies of determined Connecticut fellows of every age and appearance. Most of them were untrained yokels, some without firelocks and in shabby clothes, but they boasted to whomever would listen about how their people had captured Cape Breton without the help of British lobsterbacks, as redcoats were derisively termed. They promised to make quick work of the French and Indians, and they spoke badly of Johnson and Yorkers and Englishmen, too. Shuckburgh was a redcoat, an Englishman, and a Yorker. His dismay at hearing of Johnson's defeat was compounded by the attitude of these ignorant Connecticut Yankees.

When he arrived at Albany, it was with astonishment and joy

that he heard the first news had been all wrong, that the battle actually had been won by Johnson's army. The enemy was retreating, and their vaunted general was wounded and a prisoner. Albany was jubilant, but Shuckburgh had little time to celebrate, for there were hundreds of wounded to tend, including William Johnson, who had been shot in the hip. Much of the surgeon's work was done at the military encampment, a ramshackle scattering of dingy gray tents and bark huts on the Fort Crailo grounds across from Albany. The militia encampment resembled, as usual, a country fair more than an orderly tent-city of disciplined soldiers, though a few ambitious volunteers occasionally attempted some awkward semblance of drill.

There were even more hard feelings between Yorkers and Yankees about the performance of Lyman and Johnson. Men on either side blatantly accused the other colony's colonel of being a coward in the heat of battle. Old resentments ran as deeply as ever. Yankees snorted derisively to hear that William Johnson, as the victorious army's commander, was actually to be knighted for the triumph at Lake George, when it was Connecticut's Lyman who deserved the honor, for he had taken over after Johnson was wounded during the most desperate part of the battle. It was Lyman who had led the men to victory while Johnson was out of the fight, in his tent behind the lines, being treated for a trivial wound.

All in all, though, the mood of soldier and civilian alike around Fort Crailo was cheerful, with everyone's hope renewed by the defeat of the French and Indians. When off-duty,

Shuckburgh spent much time reveling with his friends, most of them associates of Johnson's, whose health they drank every night. Shuckburgh also visited the Van Rensselaers, who celebrated a wedding as well as a victory: their lovely daughter Katrina married the dashing Captain Philip Schuyler, an Albany patroon, who had been at the Battle of Lake George, as the engagement was named. Shuckburgh was a friend to both Dutch families, frequenting their dinner parties and balls, where his joking and clever stories were always a delight. His attitude to life was to enjoy it to the fullest, as expressed in a letter he once wrote about some temporary setback: "I endeavour to forget that and every Disappointment, being as merry as I can make myself and those about me, and I am apt to say...that I have made more People laugh in my Lifetime in the World of America than will cry at my departure out of it."

The sight of those gaunt and half-clad scarecrows of Connecticut militiamen, their awkward marching, faces and eyelids greased to keep off the flies and mosquitoes — all this made Shuckburgh and the Yorkers very merry, indeed. Soon, regular troops began arriving at Albany, many of them survivors of the Braddock campaign. Although their red coats and white smallclothes showed signs of wear, some patched where bullets or arrows had torn them, these soldiers seemed immaculately turned out by comparison with the Connecticut militiamen.

When the redcoats drilled or fired their artillery in practice, country-bred lads gathered to watch. They peered closely at the immense cannon with barrels like tree trunks, and at the squat

A charging British light dragoon of the mid-1700s.

mortars resembling half pumpkin shells, some thought. The greenhorns comically jumped en masse at the unexpected blast of guns or mortars. They were also impressed by mounted trooper exercises, with mock charges and sudden wheeling and saber slashing. Though the proud Yankees did their best to appear only mildly curious, it was not easy to hold your ground when a troop of horsemen suddenly thundered at you then pulled up to fire uncharged pistols as if you were the enemy. When puzzled young militiamen had the stupidity to ask idle questions of sweating regulars working hard at digging entrenchments, the answers they got were usually rude or teasing.

As for the militia musicians, they could not deny the skill of the regular army drummers and fifers sending out their complicated instructions to the soldiers. It was impressive to hear snare drummers beating various combinations of short and long raps as signals that told when to get up, to fetch water, to muster, to come for dinner, and when to prepare for bed. Just like his drummers, Brother Jonathan's fifers were eager to learn from the redcoats, whose smart drilling to the sound of fifes and drums thrilled anyone who had ever tried to march in step. Shuckburgh had to laugh whenever he saw the bumpkins try it.

Thinking to entertain his Dutch and English friends with a bit of doggerel poetry, Shuckburgh found a perfect theme in the antics of these determined Yankee militiamen. Of course, he knew the "Doodle-doo" tune, which by now was not just a folk song, for almost everyone in the empire had heard the version which was associated with an immensely popular English musical play called *The Beggar's Opera*. Performed by both professionals and amateurs all over the colonies, *The Beggar's Opera* delighted English America, except for New England, where play-acting was considered the devil's work and was forbidden.

Written by playwright John Gay and first performed in London in 1728, the opera was a scathingly satirical look at British society, and it fired darts at the arrogant upper classes and at government corruption. From its setting in the lower depths of criminal London, *The Beggar's Opera* offered up dark humor which was conveyed in familiar tunes that had been given new lyrics to fit the story and characters. For almost thirty years it had been the best-known show in all the British Empire. (There had even been a performance in Paris in 1750.) In America, almost every amateur performing group had put it on, and it was even secretly performed in Puritan New England — "read" in a private home rather than presented publicly on a stage.

The Beggar's Opera's songs were sung everywhere, its jests standard fare. Performers usually injected timely new gags and songs about the latest news or local topics that were sure to delight the audience. When the opera played in New York City, for example, nothing would go over better than a bit about a comic peasant who looked and sounded like "Yankee Doodle."

Shuckburgh chose that very notion as he sat down on the well curb of the Fort Crailo manor house in Green Bush to write his own teasing verses to the "Doodle-doo" song.

When he treated his dinner audience to rhymes about a gullible young Brother Jonathan coming into a military encampment, they howled with laughter. The verses were repeated and passed on, eventually heard by redcoats who heartily latched onto them. The tune was ideal for playing on a fife while tramping along, and company wits were inspired to shout out their own verses as they marched.

The "Yankey Song" was born.

> *Father and I went up to camp*
> *Along with Captain Goodwin,*
> *And there we see the men and boys*
> *As thick as hasty pudding.*
>
> *I see a man a-talking there,*
> *You might've heard to the barn, sir,*
> *Halooing and a-scolding, too,*
> *The devil if one would answer.*
>
> *He had him on his meeting clothes,*
> *Upon a slapping stallion,*
> *He set the world along in rows,*
> *There must've been a million!*
>
> *He had a ribbon on his hat,*
> *It looked so nation fine, sir!*
> *I wanted it most deucedly*
> *To give to my Jemima.*

And there I see a pumpkin shell
  As big as Mother's basin,
And every time they touched it off,
  We scampered like the nation.

I see a little barrel, too,
  The heads were made of leather,
They knocked upon't with little clubs
  To call the folks together.

The troopers, too, would gallop up
  And fire right in our faces;
It scared me almost half to death
  To see them run such races.

I see another snarl of men,
  A-digging graves, they told me,
So tarnal long, so tarnal deep,
  They 'tended they should hold me!

It scared me so, I hooked it off,
  Nor stopped, as I remember,
Nor turned about till I got home,
  Locked up in Mother's chamber.

Before the Yankees themselves ever heard his uncomplimen-
tary verses, Shuckburgh got the ear of some of their fifers and

recommended the tune to them as the most celebrated marching music in all the British Army. Before long, company after company of unwitting Jonathans were awkwardly marching to a tune that inevitably brought the mocking verses to the minds of Yorker and redcoat onlookers. The more the Yankees fifed it as they clumped back and forth on the parade ground, the funnier was the joke on them.

The sight of some gawky Jonathans sporting feathers in their hats inspired a verse that harked back to a class of posturing fops in England who dressed outrageously in lavish wigs and gaudy hats and coats and tossed words from French or Italian into their speech. These notorious dandies, with their showy taste for foreign styles and foods, were called "Macaronies." The verse told of a simple yokel thinking he looked "nation fine, sir," feeling like a dandy, though all he had done was put a feather in his hat.

> *Yankee Doodle came to town*
> *Riding on a pony,*
> *Stuck a feather in his hat*
> *And called him Macaroni.*

The danger passed at Albany and Fort Crailo, and the militia troops were sent home before winter. In time, the New Englanders learned all about the cutting verses of the "Yankey Song," whether they were Shuckburgh's words or someone else's. Hearing it became another bitter pill to them, considering all the New England blood that had been spilled in colonial wars over the years.

Like the casual British return of Fortress Louisbourg, the "Yankey Song" stung, a barb from both Yorkers and Britishers. Often when that tune was played in the presence of New Englanders, there were brawls. Being called "Brother Jonathan" was all right, but these days the name "Yankee" riled people from New England. Feelings were bad enough between individual colonies and between the colonies and the home country, but the "Yankey Song" only made things worse.

Macaroni

Fixtures of London society in the 1700s, young dandies called "Macaronies" sported extravagant garb and outrageous hair styles, such as the enormous queue hanging down the back in this period illustration.

> *Aminidab is just come home*
> *His eyes all smeared with bacon,*
> *And all the news that he could tell*
> *Is Cape Breton is taken.*

Mocking the men of the Cape Breton campaign was mean-spirited, to say the least, but when the verses toyed with the often archaic names of New Englanders, they could get too personal. For instance, one name used was Ephraim, which was the same as that of the late Colonel Ephraim Williams. A loved and respected figure in western Massachusetts and a member of the provincial congress, Williams had fallen fighting gallantly at Lake George in the victory that had covered Sir William Johnson, now known as the Mohawk Baronet, in so much glory.

> *Brother Ephraim sold his cow*
> *To buy him a commission*
> *And then he went to Canada*
> *To fight for the nation.*
>
> *But when Ephraim he came home*
> *He proved an arrant coward,*
> *He wouldn't fight the Frenchmen there*
> *For fear of being devoured.*

The sting of the "Yankey Song" was felt all over New England, and it chaffed all that much more when British troops adopted it as a favorite and added new verses, many far more vulgar than Dr. Shuckburgh's polite company at Fort Crailo would have appreciated. In the next few years, thousands of regulars came to America to fight the French and Indians, and the war turned in favor of the British. It was distressing, however, to hear the redcoat's constant disparagement of New England fighting men.

Certainly, there were notable exceptions, such as General Jeffrey Amherst, who so depended on colonial rangers led by Hampshireman Robert Rogers. There was also Colonel Thomas Gage, who at Amherst's bidding organized his own regiment of forest-fighting British regulars, called Gage's Own Light Infantry and uniformed in brown; but they never were comparable to Rogers and his men. Then there was the brilliant general, Lord George Howe, adored by Rogers Rangers, who taught him the first lessons of forest warfare, and who were revered by him in turn. Things might have turned out differently between Britain and America if Lord Howe, with his modesty and great heart, had risen to the British high command instead of being killed while on a scout with the rangers.

The most famous of all English generals in the French and Indian War had little chance to appreciate what was best in New England fighting men. Under the command of Amherst, and with the support of a great fleet, General James Wolfe led nine thousand regulars and five hundred colonials to recapture Fortress Louisbourg in 1758. As he set out on his next campaign, this time to take Quebec, Wolfe sourly remarked that "Yankees...are better for ranging and scouting than either work or vigilance," and called them "the dirtiest, most contemptible, cowardly dogs that you can conceive."

Mortally wounded in the assault on Quebec, Wolfe was told of his army's triumph, and he gasped, "I die happy."

But ignorant.

Brave Wolfe was too genteel to understand what those audacious New Englanders had done to take Louisbourg in 1745; he apparently never met a frontier militiaman the likes of Colonel Ephraim Williams, and he did not live long enough to know Rogers (Yankee) Rangers, who struck fear into French and Indians, and whose exploits were legendary in all the British Army.

Four

SONG OF VICTORY

When the second [British] brigade marched out of Boston to reinforce the first, nothing was played on the fifes and drums but "Yankee Doodle." ... Upon their return to Boston, one asked his brother officer how he liked the tune now. — "D—n them!" returned he, "they made us dance it 'till we were tired." — Since which, "Yankee Doodle" sounds less sweet to their ears.

Report in the *Massachusetts Spy,* Worcester, May 20, 1775, a few weeks after the Battle of Lexington and Concord.

OCTOBER 1, 1768. It had come to this: a fleet of royal men-of-war was anchored in Boston harbor, broadside to the city so guns could be brought to bear if the people resisted the disembarkment of the troops. Warships with flags and pennants flying covered the long-dreaded landing of six hundred British regulars, who were carried in longboats from troopship to the dock. The men stood crammed together, Brown Bess muskets held at their sides, as their boats were towed toward Boston's Long Wharf.

They had come to protect the officials of King George III, to bring peace to a troubled colony, and to strike fear into those causing unrest in Massachusetts or anywhere else in the American colonies. There were governors' homes to protect, tax collectors to defend, members of the anti-government Sons of Liberty to arrest, and treasonous rabble-rousers to bring to justice. The home government in Britain was determined to prevent open rebellion breaking out here, rebellion that could spread to the other colonies if Boston were allowed to continue its insolent hostility to the British government.

Since the end of the French and Indian War in 1763, there had been nothing but trouble between Massachusetts and Britain — oppressive trade regulations and taxation by the government, riots and boycotts of British goods by the colonists. Boston was the hotbed of American opposition to the acts of Parliament, and now was the moment to enforce order and obedience once and for all. It would be done with a heavy hand if need be, as an example to all potential rebels. These soldiers landing at Long Wharf were an occupation force. Boston had lost its liberty.

Boat by boat, the troops arrived at the wharf and assembled in smart, straight ranks. Officers gave quiet commands to sergeants who in turn bellowed the same commands to the rank and file. Snare drums rapped out signals, and voices and drums mingled with the tramp of a thousand feet, the sounds echoing off the stone walls of the houses. Long Wharf resounded with the simultaneous touch on cobblestone of six hundred musket butts, with the slap and clatter of perfect movements to bring up and shoulder the Brown Bess, with the clop of officers' prancing mounts. It was an impressive display, but there were no admiring cheers from crowds of people. Few were on hand to watch, though curtains at windows were pushed slightly open, and sullen men lounged inside alleys and doorways, glaring, angry, resentful.

The regulars came to attention, their ranks absolutely silent save for the flapping of regimental flags, which had been uncased for the coming parade through Boston. First, however, the command rang out to load firelocks, and in unison the troops executed the precise movements required to charge their muskets. This ominous loading was to demonstrate that the regulars were fully prepared for trouble. It was a show of force intended to intimidate the government's enemies in Boston and to reassure its friends. The troops again shouldered arms, and mounted officers assumed their places at the head of the long column of red and white. Drums rolled, fifes screeched, and the soldiers marched toward the heart of the city.

Ten or twenty years ago, regiments of regulars on their way to fight the French were cheered by happy crowds waving hats and handkerchiefs, holding children up on shoulders to gaze admiringly at the parade. Though troops had passed through Boston

To punish its colony of Massachusetts for opposing the laws of Parliament, the British government sent an army to occupy Boston in 1768; this period

engraving shows troops being transported from their ships to the Long Wharf as the arriving regimental bands played "Yankee Doodle" to insult Bostonians.

by the thousands during the wars against the French, and though New England had profited from the business of war and supplying armies, few citizens wanted to have a redcoat garrison here. The rank and file were mostly rough, hard men from the grittiest depths of British society. Soldiers invariably brought public drunkenness and carousing, fighting with one another and citizens, thieving and whoring. Of all the American cities, Puritan Boston had the most strict laws to keep folk pious and quiet (unless they happened themselves to be rioting against British laws considered unjust and oppressive).

Nor were most redcoats lovers of Americans, who to them were no better than scoundrels, cowards, and stupid rustic bumpkins ungrateful for all the empire had done to make them rich and secure. General Thomas Gage, commander of British forces in America, believed the presence of soldiers would finally bring order and peace to the unruly city, but most colonials were sure it would only mean more conflict, and surely bloodshed. Gage, himself, was as much a colonial as anyone, having served continuously in America since the French war of the mid-1750s. He even had married an American woman. Yet he was unwilling to believe those who warned him that Massachusetts would not be cowed by a few hundred regulars, that the colony would continue resisting bad British commercial policies, redcoats or no redcoats.

So, it had come to a war fleet lying broadside to the city, and cocky redcoats parading through the streets to the beat of drums and the music of a regimental band. As the soldiers swung along, this bleak moment for the Bostonians was made worse when the bandsmen jauntily struck up the hated "Yankey Song," which always made the redcoats grin.

> *Sheep's head and vinegar,*
> *Buttermilk and tansy,*
> *Boston is a Yankee town,*
> *Sing, "Hey, doodle dandy!"*

> *First we'll take a pinch of snuff,*
> *And then a drink of water,*
> *And then we'll say, "How do you do?"*
> *And that's a Yankee supper.*

Boston endured more years of anger and open conflict, and the redcoats were mired ever deeper in the quarrels between the colonists and the royal government.

Colonists loyal to the crown, or who were repelled by the aggressive tactics of the radicals, closed ranks; and radicals pushing for a full-scale uprising closed theirs. In the middle were the soldiers, heartily sick of garrisoning a city where it was dangerous for them to walk out alone, and where hot-tempered insults led to brawls and broken heads. Soldiers got even with the Bostonians whenever they could, intentionally infuriating them by racing horses across the Common on the sabbath; sometimes they played fifes and drums beneath church windows, making so much racket that the minister could not be heard. Those were choice occasions for raucously striking up the "Yankey Song."

Troubles deepened as the radicals became ever more dominant, the loyalists harshly suppressed. King George sent in yet more regiments, until four thousand redcoats occupied Boston, one soldier for every three inhabitants. All over the colony, civilian militias organized and trained by the thousands. They often were led by battle-hardened men who had served in the French wars, men who well knew how the regulars looked down on them, but who also knew how to fight regulars. More than one militia leader had served with Rogers Rangers.

The militias went so far as to prepare their own gunpowder and bullets, storing them just out of reach of the soldiers in Boston. Gage was resolved that if matters ever came to a head then his troops would have to get to those supplies and keep them from the militia. Not that regulars were worried about taking on a civilian army, for they believed it would be easy to brush cowardly Yankee rabble aside.

The dashing Major John Pitcairn of the British Marines spoke for many soldiers when he scoffed, "If I draw my sword but half out of my scabbard, the whole banditti of Massachusetts will run away."

Through those bitter years of military occupation, fraught with hardship and civil disobedience, civilians and soldiers came to despise each other, often clashing when they met in public houses, in back alleys, and out in the streets. There was no city police force to keep them apart, and Boston's cobblestones were stained with the blood of soldier and civilian alike.

In March 1770, hatred between redcoat and colonist became so intense that running battles broke out between gangs of civilians and off-duty soldiers. The fighting culminated in a confrontation at the State House between soldiers on guard duty and a taunting crowd throwing snowballs loaded with stones and cursing the troops as "bloodybacks" — meaning they had to be lashed to make them obey. At a critical moment, someone yelled "Present!" and the Brown Besses came up.

Then, "Fire!"

No one could prove who shouted those commands, but it was not the captain of the guard. More blood ran on the cobblestones, and five civilians died.

In 1770, after a period of open conflict between garrison soldiers and the civilians of Boston, a mob harassed a guard detachment, which opened fire, killing five men in what became known as the "Boston Massacre."

Around this time, an angry mob in New York City defied the soldiers over the issue of "Liberty Poles," erected as symbols of colonial resistance to acts of Parliament.

Four times the "Liberty Boys," as the Sons of Liberty were nicknamed, raised Liberty Poles in Manhattan, and four times soldiers tore them down. After raising the fifth pole, hundreds of Liberty Boys held a torchlight gathering to cheer the fire-breathing speech of their leader, Connecticut's Isaac Sears. Then they paraded en masse through the city, no loyalist daring to defy them, the redcoat presence too weak to offer resistance.

Like Sears, most of these so-called New York Liberty Boys were actually from Connecticut. Many Yorkers — neutral and loyal — resented a gang of radical Yankees coming into the city to bully them this way. Though the redcoat garrison did not have

In New York City, redcoats fight with Liberty Boys who are trying to prevent the soldiers from pulling down a "Liberty Pole," which was a symbol of opposition to Parliament's North American colonial policies.

the strength to battle Sears and his men, one of Manhattan's most prominent young loyalists, using words as arrows, spoke out against the Yankee toughs.

Nineteen-year-old John Vardill despised the brutal methods of the Liberty Boys, and he wrote a satirical poem called "The Procession," unsigned copies of which were one night slipped under the doors of many a loyal household in Manhattan. Vardill was considered one of the most brilliant scholars America had ever sent to Britain for an education. A minister and teacher, he soon would be a professor of natural law and philosophy at New York's King's College and assistant rector at Trinity Church. Vardill daringly mocked Sears in the poem, calling him "king" of the Liberty Boys, and accusing him of being an ignorant bumpkin with selfish ambitions of his own.

Some stanzas were set to the "Yankey Song," and often echoed the same verses sung by redcoats.

> *My Mammy, when she carried me,*
> *Dreamed of a wondrous something —*
> *She dreamed she bore a great Mushroom*
> *As large as any Pumpkin!*

Baby Sears wants to grow up to attain his own idea of success.

> *O then a great Man will be I,*
> *And all my Foes be worsted;*
> *I'll be a Lord; — and Pumpkin Pie*
> *Devour 'till I'm bursted.*

The "Yankey Song" was more than ever a flashpoint for New Englanders, especially repugnant to those from Connecticut. It was an aggressive Connecticut militia officer who was behind the Liberty Boys and Isaac Sears invading New York City: Benedict Arnold of New Haven, with his neighbor and mentor, Silas Deane, backed Sears in anti-loyalist raids intended to silence opposition to the radicals. Like many a proud New Englander, Arnold loathed the epithet "Yankee," once even challenging an English merchant ship captain who had called him a "damned Yankee" who had no manners.

They dueled with pistols. After the first round of firing left the Englishman with a slight arm wound and Arnold untouched, the Englishman was warned that if they proceeded with another round, Arnold would shoot to kill. The Englishman called it off.

On August 23, 1773, Dr. Richard Shuckburgh died in Schenectady. Ten years before his death, Shuckburgh had sold his commission in the Independent Companies, expecting to be appointed as Sir William Johnson's secretary for Indian affairs, but instead London sent out its own man to fill that post. Shuckburgh then bought a commission as surgeon in the 17th Regiment of Foot, and for a year and a half in the mid-1760s he found himself unhappily stationed far from home and family in the distant western post of Fort Detroit. Further, his officer's pay was inadequate, and he had to sell his land on the Mohawk River to make ends meet.

Shuckburgh kept his sense of humor, though, and Johnson wrote to an associate about him, saying, "You may recollect a reply of our friend Doctor Shuckburgh...when asked by an Acquaintance if he knew the name of the then appointed Governor. 'No, Faith,' says he, 'nor do I give myself any concern about it, as I shall hear him called Names enough before he is here long.'"

In 1767, Shuckburgh sold his commission in the 17th Foot and rejoined Sir William in the Mohawk Valley, employed at last as secretary for Indian affairs. He contentedly made his home with Mary in Schenectady, not far from Johnson Hall, the baronet's mansion. That year he took another trip to London, perhaps on business related to Johnson and Indian affairs. He was often in a weak financial position, however, and had to borrow money from Johnson.

Shuckburgh grew infirm quite suddenly, and on August 26, 1773, the *New York Gazetter* published his obituary: "Died, at Schenectady, last Monday, Dr. Richard Shuckburgh, a gentleman of very genteel family, and of infinite jest and humor."

The memory of Richard Shuckburgh in 1755 writing the verses of the "Yankey Song" was kept bright for years to come by the family of Philip Schuyler and by the Van Rensselaers at Fort Crailo. This tradition was also attested to by young Captain Alexander Hamilton, who married a Schuyler daughter and later served as George Washington's most trusted aide. After Shuckburgh died, his wife returned to Long Island, where she had family, and lived there until her death in 1779.

By 1774, colonial agonies had worsened as British tea was tossed into the harbors of Boston, New York, and Charleston; a royal revenue cutter was boarded and burned, and tax collectors were assaulted by mobs, tarred and feathered and driven from their homes. Active leaders of the radicals became wanted men and went into hiding. In Boston, General Gage, who had been appointed military governor of beleaguered Massachusetts, believed those leaders would have to be caught and "sent home [as] prisoners" to England for the insurrection to be quelled.

Meanwhile, debate raged in the British Parliament over American rights, but the members could find no way to ease the terrible strain between England and her North American colonies. King George, himself, considered New England to be in a state of rebellion and told his prime minister that "blows must decide." Gage was a moderate, however, and what mattered most to him was establishing a lasting peace; after all, America was his home. He did not want to

bring on a pitched battle, though he never doubted that any militia foolish enough to stand up to regulars would be destroyed. It apparently meant little to him that twenty percent of the colony's militiamen had fought in the French and Indian wars. In fact, there probably were more battle-tested veterans among the colony's fifteen to twenty thousand volunteer militia than among the regulars.

The militia conscientiously drilled and kept weapons cleaned and ready. Each company knew what it had to do if redcoats marched out of Boston in an attempt to capture munitions or to arrest leaders of the Sons of Liberty, such as Dr. Joseph Warren, John Hancock, or Samuel Adams — these last two were living in safe houses outside the city. Now and again quick cross-country marches by British troops snapped up small caches of militia ammunition, but each time troops set out the alarms went up, bells rang, and signal guns fired. The response of the militia companies was progressively quicker with each alert, and ever larger crowds of angry colonials gathered to

New York City, viewed from the southwest, about 1775.

watch the soldiers come and go, although no fighting occurred.

Late in February 1775 Gage sent two hundred and fifty men of the 64th Foot under Lt.-Colonel Alexander Leslie by boat and then by foot to Salem, where militia supplies and cannon were known to be kept in a forge. Soon after the troops left Boston, church bells rang out the alarm, and drums beat assembly. It was a damp, cold Sunday, and folk were expected to be in church, but the marching redcoats could see crowds of colonists rushing to head the column off before it reached the stores and cannon.

The soldiers entered Salem town, playing the "Yankey Song" on their fifes, attracting furious crowds on every side. Soon, hundreds of men and boys from Salem and nearby towns were walking alongside the column, exchanging insults and taunts. When the soldiers arrived at a drawbridge over a river, they found it had been raised, preventing them from crossing. Leslie demanded the bridge be let down, and when the insurgents refused, he angrily stamped his feet and swore at them. Soldiers tried to commandeer several scows tied up nearby, but Salem men got there first and broke holes in the bottoms of the boats. When an angry redcoat menaced a boatman with a bayonet, the colonial bared his chest in defiance. The soldier made a slight stab at the man and the first blood of the coming revolution was spilled.

This enraged the crowd even more. People closed in on the troops, who stood behind their steel fence of sloped bayonets. Meanwhile, more armed militia were arriving to surround the soldiers. If a fight started, it would be bloody, and the way back to the redcoat boats would be very long, indeed. When a local minister interceded to avoid bloodshed, a compromise was made: the drawbridge would be let down, the redcoats permitted to cross and march to the nearby forge. Then the troops were honor-bound to turn around immediately and go back to Boston. Lt.-Colonel Leslie's orders called for him to go to the forge, so he was determined to do that, though he knew the cannons must have been removed by now.

Leslie's soldiers formed up and marched across the bridge, soon to wheel about and tramp back again. Watching the maneuver, the people gloated with fierce pride, some shaking fists at the "lobsterbacks," the "bloodybacks," and the soldiers cursed them in return. As they marched away, however, it was not to the incendiary tune of the "Yankey Song," but to the old British favorite, "The World Turned Upside Down."

> *If ponies were men, and grass ate cows,*
> *And cats were chased into holes by the mouse...*
> *If summer were spring, and the other way 'round,*
> *Then all the world would be upside down.*

Despite Leslie's failure, or perhaps to redeem it, Gage resolved on another surprise move, this time in much greater force. His troops would capture the militia stores stockpiled at Concord, about twenty miles from Boston, and at the same time they might apprehend a rebel leader or two.

On the moonlit night of April 18, more than eight hundred regulars quietly left the city on an expedition that was to be kept absolutely secret. It was not kept secret enough, for patriot Paul

Revere and others rode out before them to raise the militia. Throughout that long night the trudging British soldiers were haunted by the distant sound of signal cannon firing the alarm, of warning bells ringing, and on the hillsides beacon fires sprang up in the darkness.

Revolution was about to begin.

The next morning was sunny and beautiful. The drums of three crack British regiments and a battalion of Marines tapped cadence as nine hundred more soldiers marched out of Boston and took the road to Concord.

With gallant young Lord Hugh Percy leading the way on a white charger, the column stepped off briskly, bayonets gleaming in the sun, two cannon rumbling behind. Lord Percy's orders were to reinforce the troops sent the night before because General Gage was concerned that the militia might be mustering in strength. Marching to the drums' steady rap, Percy's brigade passed house after house that was shut up and silent, as if empty. Few people were to be seen. Despite the fine weather, the mood in these deserted villages was foreboding, as of an approaching storm.

A command rang out. The tap-tap of drums abruptly changed to lively crashes, and the regimental bandsmen put mouthpieces to their lips. There came a burst of familiar music, and the troops roared with laughter to hear the "Yankey Song." Someone called out the first line of a well-known verse, and hundreds of soldier voices rose to mock Brother Jonathan — or

"Yankee John," as some said — and his rebellious leaders, Hancock, Warren, and Adams:

> *Yankee Doodle came to town*
> *For to buy a firelock.*
> *We will tar and feather him,*
> *And so we will John Hancock.*

The redcoats were eager for one truly decisive fight to teach the militia a lesson they would never forget. One of the mounted scouting parties might even collar Hancock and Adams, known to be lurking in the vicinity and plotting treason. In the old days, treason was punished with beheading, and the head was displayed on a pole for all to see. Some soldiers thought Beacon Hill in Boston well suited for just such a pole.

> *As for their king, that John Hancock,*
> *And Adams, if they're taken,*
> *Their heads for signs shall hang up high*
> *Upon that hill called Beacon.*

Mile after mile, the redcoats sang out "Yankee Doodle" as company wits made up new stanzas.

> *Dolly Bushel let a fart,*
> *Jenny Jones, she found it,*
> *Ambrose carried it to the mill,*
> *Where Doctor Warren ground it.*

Mistress Hancock dreamed a dream;
She dreamed she wanted something.
She dreamed she wanted a Yankee king
To crown him with a pumpkin.

At mid-afternoon, Percy's column entered the village of Lexington. The troops fell silent when they saw bandaged soldiers from the first column being transported back to Boston in a carriage. There was blood on Lexington green, where a few hours ago the first expedition had exchanged shots with a band of militiamen. No one knew who had started it, but eight colonials had been killed, a few regulars wounded. There was no sign of dead or wounded Americans, who had been carried away by villagers, but the sound of weeping came from houses near the green. Insurrection had a price.

The bandsmen struck up another tune, and the redcoats continued their march toward Concord, less than eight miles away. Before long, distant gunfire could be heard. It was scattered but steady, obviously coming from hundreds of muskets. Scouts rode in to report that at least two thousand militia were under arms out there, hundreds more arriving. Lord Percy ordered his men and cannon deployed for action. Drums beating, the troops swiftly extended ranks across the Concord road and into adjoining fields. They prepared to advance, bayonets sloped, toward the firing, but then a crowd of soldiers from the first expedition appeared, running down the road from Concord. To the shock of Percy's men, some of these fellows were without their caps, others without muskets, and many were wounded. It was actually a retreat! How could that be? Regulars fleeing from Yankee Doodle militia?

Percy's ranks opened to let the fugitives through, but then an even larger mass of redcoats from the first brigade came into sight. They were panic-stricken, rushing pell-mell along the road. Hundreds of soldiers were hurrying toward Percy's force, and as they retreated, their rear guard stopped from time to time to fire volleys at a huge mass of militia soldiery following close behind them. Percy's guns opened fire, and the swarm of colonials scattered into the woods and fields, virtually disappearing. Soon, the redcoats could see quick movements along hedgerows, in groves of trees. Like shadows, hundreds of men were slipping from cover to cover, outflanking the regulars. Musketry flashed from bushes as the concealed militiamen fired at the exposed troops then darted to the next shelter and fired again. The windows of nearby houses began to give off puffs of smoke, where rebels had taken positions.

The last redcoats fleeing from Concord scurried into Percy's ranks, lugging their wounded and hunching low to escape the hail of musket balls. The militiamen had been shooting at the first expedition all the way from Concord, clearly trying to wipe it out, which would have happened if Percy had not arrived just in time. This was no disorderly mob action he faced. Instead, he was in danger of being surrounded and cut off by thousands of armed and determined militiamen. Taking command of all the troops, he prepared to fight his way, mile by mile, back to Boston.

Harassed on every side by angry Massachusetts militia, British soldiers retreat from the expedition to Lexington and Concord on April 19, 1775.

The redcoats began to withdraw in good order toward Boston, but the fighting became more intense, even desperate, and at times merciless. Marching in the road under hissing, zinging bullets, the soldiers fell on every side. Stragglers were cut off and shot down. Overbold colonials who ventured too close to the troops were counterattacked by flanking parties, who gave no quarter and asked none in return. Soldiers forced their way into houses where militia were forted up and firing out the windows at them. In one house, ten colonials were surrounded by angry redcoats and died to the last man under the bayonet. In another house, eight militiamen were trapped and killed after a furious fight to the death.

Flanking parties of redcoats searched every building for hidden snipers. As one squad left a house they had thought was empty, there came a rattle of musketry from the windows. The enraged soldiers turned and charged in, killing the three people who had fired at them. One was a young woman. More than once, the mere appearance of a face at a window attracted gunfire from the soldiers, who killed an unarmed boy that way.

The rebels gave far worse than they got, making that road an utter hell for the retreating troops. The air was full of hissing lead, and carts carrying wounded soldiers were so torn by bullets that their wheels collapsed, tumbling out the men. All afternoon the redcoats had to fight from house to house, orchard to graveyard, field to stone wall, but they were running out of ammunition. At Menotomy, seven miles from Boston, one of Percy's supply wagons from the city was waylaid by a gang of old men, veterans of the French and Indian wars. The drivers and guards fled for their lives, so terrified — legend has it — that six of them surrendered to a startled old woman, begging her for protection.

Hundreds more militia arrived at Menotomy to lie in wait until the column of retreating soldiers appeared and began to pass through the town. The militia fired a withering, close-range fusillade that was the worst so far. The fighting again became hand to hand, house to house, and the British struggled their way through the town in the bloodiest hour of the day. Percy had a button clipped off by a bullet, but he remained mounted even though he was a conspicuous target, resolutely leading his men out of this hell.

The British regimental bandsmen had long before fallen silent, too dismayed to play their instruments or too busy with their battlefield duty of attending to the wounded. No "Yankey Song" had been heard from them or any other redcoat since the retreat began. Late that afternoon, however, when the battle was clearly won and lost, and the British were in sight of their lines near Charlestown, there came a moment when the tune of the "Yankey Song" drifted over the embattled road. The cheerful sound of fifes playing it carried above the bark of muskets, the constant whine of bullets, and the shouts and groans of fighting men. It was not the fifes of the regulars, however, but some militia company was defiantly marching to that tune. For the first time ever, the "Yankey Song" sounded good to New Englanders.

Then, apparently recalling the soldier verse mocking John Hancock and his wife, a rebel shouted at the retreating redcoats,

"King Hancock forever!" Other militiamen cheered at that and raised the same cry. "King Hancock forever!" was roared, over and over, and soon the "Yankey Song" was being whistled by companies of militia marching to occupy stone walls or rail fences and sung by unseen colonials fighting from behind hedgerows and the cover of woods. It was heard on all sides as the militia repaid the defeated regulars with their own song, which had lost all its power to insult New Englanders.

To the astonishment of the redcoats and the joy of the battle-weary colonials in those final hours of the fight, the strains of the "Yankey Song" rose from hundreds of hoarse and weary voices in celebration of victory. Now the militiamen felt immense pride in the name, Yankee, for it would always remind them how they stood up to the king's arrogant regulars and drove them, humbled, all the way back to Boston.

One of several "Join or Die" symbols calling for the thirteen American colonies to unite against the British government.

By the time the shattered redcoat regiments stumbled exhausted and bloodied into Charlestown that evening, seventy-three had died, one hundred and seventy-four were wounded, and twenty-six were missing or prisoners. Militia losses were forty-nine dead, thirty-nine wounded, and five missing.

In Boston soon after, a heartsick British officer asked another what he thought of the "Yankey Song" now. "Damn them!" the other grumbled, dejected, and said he hoped never to hear that song again, for the Yankees "made us dance to it 'till we were tired."

The "Yankey Song" soon would have new words and a new name: "Yankee Doodle," America's song of triumph.

A TUNE FOR FIGHTING

Indeed, not only the name of a Yankee, but of a Connecticut man in particular, is become very respectable this way.

Silas Deane of New Haven, writing home to his wife on June 3, 1775, while serving as a delegate from Connecticut to the Continental Congress in Philadelphia; Deane soon would become America's agent to France, obtaining a supply of arms crucial to the Continental Army's survival.

> *When Yankies skill'd in martial rule,*
> *First put the British troops to school;*
> *Instructed them in warlike trade,*
> *And new maneuvers of parade,*
> *The true war dance of Yanky-reels,*
> *And val'rous exercise of heels.*

From *M'Fingal,* a 3,000-line, pro-Revolution epic published in Philadelphia in 1775 and composed by John Trumbull, poet and jurist born in Westbury, Connecticut.

JUNE 17, 1775. When the first gray of dawn glowed over Boston harbor, the Americans in their freshly dug earthworks on Breed's Hill thought they had been betrayed. Their position was a trap.

Last night these thousand or so militiamen from Massachusetts and Connecticut had hurried here under cover of darkness and began building defensive works, intending to shock the redcoats when they awoke in their bunks over in Boston. Instead, it was the rebel militia who were shocked when daylight came, finding themselves on a gentle slope well out on the Charlestown peninsula. They should have been back on the higher ground of Bunker's Hill, closer to the mainland. In the darkness, no one had realized how vulnerable they were to a British attack on their rear, blocking their escape to the mainland.

Some militia commander had blundered or, worse, had betrayed them, for the position they had worked on all through the night, digging and pickaxing, was impossible to hold. If the militiamen stayed here more than a few hours, they surely would be cut off and starved out. The men were already hungry, for there had been little food that night, only rations of rum. Although after Lexington and Concord thousands of militia had mustered to besiege the British in Boston — the main body of rebel troops was stationed on the mainland — there was no efficient organization to deliver either food or ammunition to the

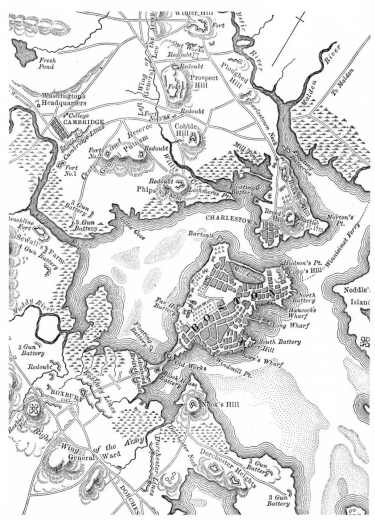

Boston and environs in 1775, showing American positions, including Washington's headquarters at Cambridge and artillery on Dorchester Heights.

Charlestown peninsula. What supplies the men had carried with them to Breed's Hill was all they could depend upon.

They had come out here full of confidence last night, knowing that other momentous events were taking place elsewhere in the northern colonies. For one, Benedict Arnold of Connecticut and Ethan Allen of the Hampshire Grants had surprised and captured the once-powerful Lake Champlain forts of Ticonderoga and Crown Point. New England and New York militias were advancing northward to join Arnold and Allen for an invasion of Canada. The northern army would be directed by Philip Schuyler of Albany, who had been named one of four top generals by the Continental Congress in Philadelphia.

A boom and a puff of smoke told that a British warship was first to spot the earthworks on Breed's Hill. The swarm of Americans paused to watch the cannonball bounce harmlessly past, and then they turned back to wielding shovel and pick. They threw up the earthen walls of a three-sided redoubt, and to the right and left prepared other lines of entrenchments and reinforced rail fences. Other ships began to fire at them, without much effect at first, although an unlucky fellow was struck by a cannonball and had to be hastily buried.

The rebels continued to work despite their doubts. Every man knew that five thousand of King George III's redcoats soon would be called to arms in Boston. British cannon over in the city on Copp's Hill next opened up against the redoubt. The militia kept on digging, alert for bouncing "iron beans," as some called cannonballs, and watching the arcing trajectories of explosive shells as they soared high and then dropped down on the earthworks. Whether the militia had been betrayed or an inexperienced commander was responsible for their precarious position, they were here and intended to stay until ordered out.

There was little sign of regulars moving on the Boston wharfs as the rebels dug furiously all that morning under worsening artillery fire and a bright June sun. By midday, many small groups of welcome reinforcements had arrived from the mainland, but there was still no sign of redcoats until early afternoon, when a flood of red filled the wharfs on the Boston side of the Charles River. Soon, troops began to clamber into barges and whaleboats to be ferried across.

It was surprising to the militia that the British seemed to be coming directly over and not, as expected, making for the neck of land that joined the peninsula to the mainland. Boatload after boatload of regulars crossed over the Charles and emptied men onto the shore below the earthworks. Redcoat drums beat, flags fluttered, cannons boomed from the ships and the battery on Copp's Hill, but no troops were moving to strike the rebels from the rear. Clearly, the British still had only scorn for the New England militia, and they intended to display it. Even after the slaughter of Lexington and Concord, military governor Thomas Gage and his three new generals just arrived from England intended to sweep the rebels from Breed's Hill with one well-executed bayonet charge and break the siege — sometimes called "the blockade" — of Boston. That would avenge the April nineteenth humiliation of the redcoats.

Those three generals were Sir William Howe, who disapproved of British colonial policies that had brought on the war; Sir Henry Clinton, born in America and ambitious for overall command; and John Burgoyne, a bon vivant playwright, dragoon commander, and confidant of the king.

The generals had arrived May 25, the very same day as the first article ever about the meaning of the newly fascinating term "Yankee" was published in the *Pennsylvania Evening Post*. Entitled "Etymology of the Word Yankee" and written tongue-in-cheek, it asserted that years ago a warlike tribe of New England Indians called "Yankoos," supposedly meaning "invincible," had held out to the last against the whites. When faced with final defeat, the Yankoos transferred their own name to the conquerors — presumably a unique custom of theirs, for it was unknown among other Indian peoples.

The *Evening Post* went on about the New Englanders: "For a while they were called Yankoos; but from a corruption, common to names in all languages, they got through time the name of Yankees. A name which we hope will soon be equal to that of a Roman, or an ancient Englishman." This article was reprinted in other publications, and so began widespread speculation on the origin of "Yankee," which was swiftly transforming in meaning from a New England "bumpkin" to a revolutionary patriot and fast becoming known by all who were watching the dangerous military situation known as the "Blockade of Boston."

The three generals had sailed to Boston aboard the HMS *Cerberus* — ironically the name of the mythical three-headed

dog that guarded the gates of Hades. An American wit immediately wrote about them:

> *Behold the Cerberus, the Atlantic plough.*
> *Her precious cargo, Burgoyne, Clinton, Howe.*
>
> > *Bow, wow, wow.*

When HMS *Cerberus* and her three military heads had
departed England, there were those in the government there
who doubted the generals' ability, and someone remarked for
posterity: "Our Generals may terrify the enemy, they certainly
terrify me." None of them was prepared for what awaited in
America.

If the generals and Gage had little experience in either breaking a rebel siege or quelling rebellion, there was one great advantage on their side: this was the courage of the regular, who would
storm hell for the sake of his regimental honor. The generals
counted on this courage, the regulars were sworn to it, and the
Yankees fully expected to face it. Watching from their shallow
Breed's Hill earthworks, they saw those scores of barges come
across the Charles and unload company after company of king's
troops. If the rebels abruptly conceded the error of their place-
ment and hastily withdrew to the higher ground of Bunker's
Hill, it would have made perfect military sense. But when it
became apparent that the British troops, with Howe at their
head, fully intended to make a frontal assault, the odds tilted in
favor of the militia.

Moreover, since the British meant to insult them by arrogantly coming up the slope into the teeth of the defense, the Americans resolved to defy them. Yankees had already proven themselves formidable when fighting from earthworks against mighty Fortress Louisbourg. Despite their vulnerable position on Breed's Hill, they had faith in their field commanders: William Prescott of Massachusetts, Israel Putnam of Connecticut, and John Stark, the former Rogers Ranger from New Hampshire. They would take on the regulars, head to head.

They kept on digging.

Artillery from the ships and the Copp's Hill battery (these guns commanded by Burgoyne) fired a steady barrage at the militia, who still dug and dug as the British troops poured onto the peninsula. By mid-afternoon twenty-five hundred regulars were formed up in long, straight ranks at the bottom of the slope. The British had fired red-hot cannonballs and exploding shells at pretty Charlestown, soon setting it ablaze. They meant to take advantage of the wind by sending clouds of smoke from the burning town across the slope to offer the redcoats conceal-ment as they attacked. By the time the troops were ready to advance, however, the wind changed and the smoke was blown the other way. That mattered little to the soldiers. They wanted only the chance to get into the rebel earthworks with the bayo-net and exact revenge for their losses at Lexington and Concord.

The troops could almost taste victory as commands to advance rang out across the peninsula. They were heavily laden, carrying three days' rations, full kit, ammunition, knapsacks, and blankets — so this would not be a rapid assault. Up the hill went the slow tide of red and white, flags flying, drums beating, fifes playing favorite regimental tunes, including "Yankee Doodle." The redcoats were determined not to give it up to the rebels, no matter what had happened on the Lexington Road. The British Army now used "Yankee Doodle" as its "rogue's march," music that was played when a soldier guilty of some crime was punished, shamed, or drummed out of the regiment in full view of his paraded fellow soldiers.

The advance of the long ranks of redcoats was a slow, relentless wave climbing the slope. The sight was enough to instill fear in any enemy, and many soldiers expected the Yankees to break and run at any moment, scattering like ants from their hill. In the redoubt, the grim rebels waited, no one firing a shot, but the American drummers and fifers rang out their own defiant "Yankee Doodle," which some called "The Lexington March." The rebels were putting new words to the tune, and these were not all in the spirit of the country boy's humorous visit to camp.

> *Yankee Doodle is the tune,*
> *That we all delight in;*
> *It suits for feasts, it suits for fun,*
> *And just as well for fighting!*

The militiamen stared, transfixed, at the mass of redcoats coming ever closer. Orders were to wait until the British front ranks advanced up and over the brow of the slope, letting their caps come into full view, then their chests with the white cross belts, then their legs, until the top button on their gaiters could be seen.

A storm of fire roared down, point-blank on the regulars, who reeled, falling in swaths. Massed rebel musketry staggered the entire battle line. The troops wavered, fired back, tried to keep order, discipline, tried to organize for a bayonet charge, but the Americans fired and fired without letup, gusts of flame and smoke and hissing ball made the regulars recoil, their lead officers wiped out, whole companies going down where they stood, wounded and dying in ranks, until at last — on direct orders — they retreated back down the hill, decimated and shaken.

The jubilant, powder-blackened rebels cheered, as astonished as they were elated. They had stood their ground against some of the finest troops in the British Army and had repelled them. The slaughter was horrific. The slope was covered with redcoats, scores lying dead, many writhing in agony, some trying to crawl away, others staggering from the stricken field, leaning on comrades who also were wounded.

Once again, British arrogance had cost the valiant line troops and their officers dearly. It was a brutal repulse, a defeat — or so it seemed at first to the Americans. Soon, however, it became apparent the redcoats were not finished yet. Their officers were gesticulating with swords, keeping men from clambering back into the boats, and before long the ranks were forming to come on once more. Again in straight lines, as if on parade, they advanced in perfect order up that bloody slope, resolute and stoic, many bandaged and bleeding, anticipating the moment when they would be commanded to fire a volley and rush the American works.

Before that moment came, the rebels fired, obliterating the front ranks, the slaughter as terrible as before. The redcoats tried to stand but were unable to advance, stubbornly unwilling to retreat. Firing and loading by ranks, they fell in clusters of red and white. Officers suffered the most, pacing in front of their men, heedless of the storm of lead. At last, the redcoats had to retreat again, and the Americans roared in triumph.

If ever Yankees had proven their mettle, it was now, face to face with troops famous for bayonet charges that shattered trained European soldiery. The rebels had driven them.

The battle had raged for almost an hour and a half. Breed's Hill was littered with hundreds of dead and wounded soldiers, testimony to the British again underestimating the Americans. Even redcoat valor could not make up for such a mistake. American losses were light so far. It would not remain that way for long. The regulars were throwing off heavy knapsacks, coats, and extra gear. They were reorganizing.

They were coming on again.

British field artillery took new positions to rake the entrenchments outside the redoubt, and the Americans there were forced to withdraw. The men in the redoubt prepared to meet the brunt of a third assault, but they were asking one another for powder, for ball. Their ammunition was almost gone, few with more than four rounds left. If the British endured the first blasts and got into the earthworks, most rebels did not have bayonets for hand-to-hand combat.

British artillery kept bombarding the entrenchments.

The redcoats would do or die this time. So would the Yankees, who leaned forward on the redoubt's earthen walls and waited. Some had only one shot left, but they would stay to deliver it, no matter how close the cold steel came. They would not run.

The soldiers attacked, charging.

The Americans again waited until the last possible moment and fired. The redcoats staggered, many falling, but the rest stood it out under the first fury of the rebel blasts. They reformed, fired back, and some dashed forward to huddle in groups against the earthworks, briefly concealed from the American muskets above. Then the defenders' firing slowed, sputtered, and went "out like an old candle." The British knew this was their moment. They clambered up and over the redoubt, bayonets flashing. The Americans fought back desperately with musket butt and fists until they had to back off and then flee from the redoubt, now filled with redcoats. As the rebels scattered, several companies made stands to allow the main body to escape. John Stark and his Hampshiremen, who refused to turn their backs on the enemy, carried out a stubborn, fighting retreat.

As for the British, bloodied and exhausted, their fury spent in the final bayonet assault on the redoubt, they were given no orders for hot pursuit of the retreating rebels. They had won the field, but at the cost of two hundred and twenty-six dead and more than a thousand wounded — half the attacking force. About four hundred Americans were killed, wounded, or cap-

The Battle of Breed's Hill from behind British lines, looking up at the New England militiamen in their earthen redoubt at the top of the slope.

tured. Among the dead was Dr. Joseph Warren, president of the provincial council and the subject of vulgar redcoat verses to "Yankee Doodle." Recently appointed a militia general, Warren could have been safe at headquarters today, but he chose to come to Breed's Hill and fight as a volunteer in the redoubt.

The battle, known as Bunker Hill, did nothing to break the blockade of Boston. The city was once again a sorrowful charnel house filled with dead and wounded soldiers. A Philadelphia newspaper reported that "General Gage's troops are much dispirited...and...disposed to leave off dancing any more to the tune of Yankey Doodle."

The tenacity and courage of the Americans, who stood and fought to the very last, dismayed the British government and high command, and the name "Yankee" rose ever higher in esteem. One of the redcoats who had taken part in the battle wrote a ballad that praised the British soldiers who fought for Breed's Hill; it could be sung to the tune of "Yankee Doodle."

> *On the seventeenth by break of day,*
> *The Yankees did surprise us,*
> *With their strong works they had thrown up*
> *To burn the town and drive us.*
>
> *But soon we had an order come,*
> *An order to defeat them,*

> *Like rebels stout they stood it out*
> *And thought we ne'er could beat them.*

As is to be expected, the song celebrates the valor of the British regular, but by admitting that it required so great an effort to drive the New Englanders from Breed's Hill, it also conceded the valor of the defenders:

> *Brave William Howe on our right wing*
> *Cried, "Boys, fight on like thunder;*
> *You soon will see the rebels flee*
> *With great amaze and wonder."*

Indeed, the rebels had reason to be amazed — but amazed at their ability to face three redcoat assaults before retreating, protected by rearguard actions.

In his memoirs, a young British officer described the rebel mood, saying that after "the affair at Bunker's Hill, the Americans gloried" in being called Yankees, and "Yankee Doodle is now their paean, a favourite of favourites, played in their army, esteemed as warlike as the Grenadier's March — it is the lover's spell, the nurse's lullaby."

In time, the rebel camp was much heartened despite its own grievous losses. A new pride surged in the militiamen, who expected soon the arrival of reinforcements from other colonies and a general commissioned by the Continental Congress.

On July 2, George Washington, newly appointed commander-in-chief of the Continental Army, arrived in Cambridge after a long journey from Philadelphia, riding on horseback across New Jersey and through New York City and Connecticut to Massachusetts. A Virginian who, twenty years earlier, had risen to be a colonel of provincial forces, Washington had limited military experience, but he coolly undertook the daunting task of organizing and disciplining the unmilitary volunteers. There was no staff and no cash.

Facing confusion, resentment, and insolence at every turn, Washington found indifference and disrespect for authority in some officers. Mutiny threatened among the men, who had been too many weeks away from home. Further, there was not enough black powder if the army had to meet a strong British attempt at breaking out. Washington was resolved to keep his

View of the Town of BOSTON

troops "watchful and vigilant," but he had to appeal to "Brother Jonathan" — the people of New England — for a supply of gunpowder from their private stores. When troubles reached a crisis, he broke some officers in rank and gave others new responsibilities. Preparing to maintain the siege through the coming winter, Washington faced down potential mutineers and had men punished for insubordination; when many left the Cambridge camp after their enlistments were up, he somehow held together enough of a force to continue the siege.

eeds Hill in CHARLESTOWN.

It was a consolation that things were far worse in blockaded Boston, where every day people fell dead on the streets from disease and hunger. In the city it came to eating horses, dogs, and eventually rats. Added to the distress of the British and to the hopes of the Americans was news that a rebel army had captured Montreal and that Quebec, too, was besieged. Coordinated

A contemporary view of Boston, across the Charles River, as seen from Breed's Hill, where the American militia built earthworks.

by Schuyler, that expedition was led by the gallant Irish-born former British officer, Richard Montgomery, who lived in the Hudson Valley, and was supported by Benedict Arnold.

As winter approached, those allied Yorkers and Yankees had made dramatic progress against the king's forces in Canada, where the French Canadians preferred to keep out of the fight. Among the young rebel officers in the Canadian campaign was nineteen-year-old Aaron Burr of New Jersey, who spoke fluent French and was welcomed to partake of food and shelter in the home of a "merry old" French-Canadian woman and her pretty daughters, as he described it. When Burr announced that he and his comrades had trekked all the way from Boston, the old woman laughed and "immediately fell to singing and dancing Yankee Doodle with the greatest air of good humor."

Bitterness at rebel successes made a loyalist writer lampoon Washington in verses set to "Yankee Doodle" and entitled "Adam's Fall."

> *When Congress sent great Washington,*
> *All clothed in powder and breeches,*
> *To meet old Britain's warlike sons*
> *And make some rebel speeches.*
>
> *'Twas then he took his gloomy way*
> *Astride his dapple donkeys,*
> *And travelled well, both night and day,*
> *Until he reached the Yankees.*

Full many a child went into camp,
All dressed in homespun kersey,
To see the greatest rebel scamp
That ever crossed o'er Jersey.

The rebel clowns, oh! what a sight!
Too awkward was their figure;
'Twas yonder stood a pious wight,
And here and there a nigger.

Late in 1775, a Philadelphia publisher produced the epic poem *M'Fingal,* a three-thousand-line work that satirized loyalists through the character of conservative Squire M'Fingal, who supports the British government.

Written by young John Trumbull of Westbury, Connecticut, *M'Fingal* made one of the first published commentaries on the song "Yankee Doodle," as Squire M'Fingal ironically boasts about British redcoats:

Did not our troops show much discerning
And skill your various arts in learning?
Outwent they not each native Noodle
By far in playing Yanky-doodle;
Which, as 'twas your New England tune,
'Twas marvellous they took so soon?

But the narrator in *M'Fingal* says something else:

> *When Yankies skill'd in martial rule,*
> *First put the British troops to school;*
> *Instructed them in warlike trade,*
> *And new maneuvers of parade,*
> *The true war dance of Yanky-reels,*
> *And val'rous exercise of heels.*

Then the narrator recalls the battle on the Concord and Lexington Road, twenty miles of defeat and retreat for the British:

> *And ere the year was fully thro',*
> *Did they not learn to foot it, too?*
> *And such a dance as ne'er was known,*
> *For twenty miles on end lead down.*

In 1775-76 the verses set to the "Yankee Doodle" tune were as varied as those who made them up, sang, and marched to them. Some verses were better known than others, and the American camp at Cambridge, where Washington had his headquarters, often heard the following sung — the first remarking on Washington's stable of five magnificent horses he had bred himself and brought north from Virginia:

> *There was Captain Washington*
> *Upon a spanking stallion,*

And all the people standing 'round —
There must've been a million!

The flaming ribbons in his hat,
They looked so tarnal fine, sir,
I wanted peskily to get
To give to my Jemima.

And there we see a thousand men
As rich as Squire David,
And what they wasted every day —
I wish it could be savèd.

Uncle is a Yankey man,
I'faith, he pays us all off,
And he has got a fiddle that's
As big as Daddy's hog trough.

There is a man in our town,
I pity his condition,
He sold his oxen and his sheep
To buy him a commission.

This last might have been one of the original Shuckburgh verses, for unlike redcoats, American militia officers did not buy their commissions, but were elected by their companies. Elected officers made military discipline difficult, of course, for they were considered equals with their men. Too many militiamen

Shortly after the battle on Breed's Hill, General George Washington arrived at Cambridge to take command of the militia army in the name of the Continental

Congress; Washington was famous for the handsome, "spanking stallions" (sometimes "slapping") he brought with him from Virginia.

obeyed only when it suited them, and they invariably objected to being told what to do by any officer they had not elected themselves.

In the "Yankey Song" the young bumpkin militiaman and his father cautiously step up close to look at the "underpinnings," or foundations, of a "swamping" — impressive, remarkable — field cannon.

> *And then they had a swamping gun*
> *As big's a log of maple,*
> *Put upon two little wheels,*
> *A load for Father's cattle.*
>
> *I went as near to it myself*
> *As Jacob's underpinning,*
> *And Father went as near again,*
> *I thought the deuce was in him.*

In camp, home-cooked or home-grown food often was acquired by trading with locals, such as "Uncle Sam," who wants molasses cakes — a sugar staple — from the soldiers. (Just as older black women were often called "Aunty," older black men were sometimes known as "Uncle.")

> *Old Uncle Sam come there to change*
> *Some pancakes and some onions*
> *For 'lasses-cakes to carry home*
> *To give his wife and young ones.*

Christmas is a-coming, boys,
We'll go to Mother Chase's
And there we'll get a sugar dram
Sweetened with molasses.

Oftimes it was "Uncle Chase's," but both loyalist and rebel Yankee could appreciate this stanza about a "sugar dram," a glass of whiskey or rum sweetened with molasses and sometimes called a "Yankee Doodle." Likewise, Dutch Yorkers still called a glass of gin a "Jan Doodle." The New Englanders were pleased to call Boston a Yankee town.

Sheep's head and vinegar,
Buttermilk and tansy,
Boston is a Yankee Town,
Sing, "Hey Doodle Dandy!"

Around this time a delightful new refrain came to be, one that was more appealing than the often-used two-line chorus:

Doodle doodle doo,
Pa, pa, pa, pa, pa.

The new refrain harked back to the fun of dancing to "Yankee Doodle," sometimes called "Yankee Tootle" or "Yankee Doodle-doo." Most of all, this refrain expressed the surging, newfound pride of the rebel New Englander.

Yankee Doodle keep it up,
Yankee Doodle Dandy!

Mind the music and the step,
And with the girls be handy.

Eventually, General Washington became utterly disgusted by the casual, lighthearted attitude of so many of his soldiers as they drilled to the sound of fifes and drums. He demanded stricter discipline and ordered that "only the 'Quick Step' [was] to be played, with such moderation that the men may step to it with ease — without dancing along, as too often has been their wont."

ANTHEM OF REVOLUTION

Cornwallis led a country dance,
The like was never seen, sir,
Much retrograde and much advance,
And all with General Greene, sir.

His music soon forgets to play —
His feet can no more move, sir,
And all his bands now curse the day,
They jiggèd to our shore, sir.

From "Cornwallis's Country Dance," by an anonymous author; sung
(or jigged) to the tune of "Yankee Doodle," it parodies the Southern
campaign of Britain's Lord Cornwallis, who opposed General
Nathanael Greene until cornered and captured at Yorktown in
October 1781.

J ANUARY 8, 1776. Under the cheery glow of candelabra, British officers costumed as women — some as ladies of the night — stepped onto a makeshift stage in Faneuil Hall to entertain fellow officers and some real ladies. To the laughter and applause of the audience, the actors enthusiastically performed a humorous musical farce entitled *The Blockade of Boston,* written by General John Burgoyne.

The play was meant to lift the spirits of besieged soldier and loyalist Bostonian alike, caricaturing Washington as a fat oaf in a huge wig, with a long sword that inevitably trips him up. "Play-acting," however, was considered a sin in Boston. Many loyalists trapped in the city were outraged that stately Faneuil Hall, Boston's most important public meeting place, had been turned into a theater. Laws in New England forbade public theatricals, and over the years stiff penalties had been imposed on those few daring enough to attempt to produce a play for an audience. Debauchery, exaggerated pride, serving as the devil's tool, depravedly dressing up in costumes, men wearing women's clothes — these, to most Bostonians, were the sins of play-acting.

Redcoats and their audience of families and friends thought differently. At home in England, where the theater was a popular and much-loved entertainment, amateur acting troupes put on plays all over the country. In fact, this was also the case in most of America these days; it was mainly New England, with

its Puritanical roots, that absolutely forbade acting on penalty of
fine and imprisonment. They could not fine the British Army,
however, so Burgoyne's show went on, to the delight of the war-
weary audience glittering under the candles of Faneuil Hall.
Though the Americans had the British firmly pinned in Boston,
these redcoats were determined to hold out and make the most
of their situation.

By the time *The Blockade of Boston* was performed, Burgoyne
had already gone back to England to press his case with the king
for a field command of his own, and he missed the pleasure these
friends and comrades found in his broad humor. Near the play's
conclusion, a character named "Doodle" spouts invective at
rebellious New England "prigs." He declares them too tyrannical to call themselves Whigs, members of the liberal political
party that championed popular rights and opposed the Tories,
the party in power in Britain:

> *Ye tar-barrell'd Lawgivers, Yankified Prigs,*
> *Who are Tyrants in Custom, yet call yourselves Whigs;*
> *In return for the Favors you've lavished on me,*
> *May I see you all hang'd upon Liberty Tree.*
> *Mean Time take Example, decease from Attack,*
> *You're as weak under Arms as I'm weak in my Back.*
> *In War and in Love we alike are betray'd,*
> *And alike are the Laughter of BOSTON BLOCKADE.*

Over the years, Faneuil Hall had held fiery political meetings, official ceremonies, and cheerful banquets, but it had never rocked with laughter as it did when the redcoats put on a farce like this. The audience howled to see a redcoat sergeant suddenly burst onstage from the wings, eyes wide, yelling, "Turn out! Turn out! They're hard at it, hammer and tongs!"

They loved it, cheering and clapping at his performance, which was all the more hilarious because he kept jumping up and down, his voice drowned out by the noise of the audience. When the applause finally stopped, the sergeant bellowed at the hall full of his superior officers:

"What the deuce are you all about? If you won't believe me, by Jaysus, then you need only go to the door, and then you'll see and hear, both!"

They did.

Gunfire crackled across the harbor, and flashes lit the night sky. A rebel attack was underway somewhere, and the sound of British drums told that the garrison was indeed turning out. To the anguish of the ladies, who would have to find their own way home that night, the officers of both audience and cast bolted away to join their units. The actors reached their posts with faces still painted, a few in costume dresses, petticoats flying. The raid turned out to be a minor one, and some believed the Yankee rebels knew this scandalous play-acting was going on and so opened fire on British positions just to disrupt the performance.

It required much more than a silly play and an occasional enemy raid to relieve the boredom of the unhappy redcoats garrisoning beleaguered Boston. The soldier's life here was bleak, with little shelter to be found when on duty in the entrenchments of the forward lines or on the various islands where troops were needed to protect lighthouses, beef cattle, and important loyalist estates. In the city, food was short for everyone, tables not at all in keeping with the lavishness expected by many a gentleman staff officer.

The Yankees all around were a constant threat, raiding and harrying on land and on water, sniping at sentries, and showing no sign of giving up their siege. Nor were they overawed by Burgoyne's wit. Some anonymous rebel sympathizer — possibly poet Mercy Otis Warren, sister of leading revolutionary James Otis — wrote a play in reply to Burgoyne's *The Boston Blockade* and called it *The Blockheads, or The Affrighted Officers*. The leading British officers, from Lord Percy to Burgoyne, were portrayed and given appropriate stage names, such as Lord Dapper, Shallow, and Surly.

The prologue set a sarcastic tone and expressed the essence of rebel New England's thinking in those days:

> *By Yankees frightened, too! Oh, dire to say!*
> *Why, Yankees sure at Red-coats faint away!*
> *Oh, yes! they thought so, too, for lackaday,*
> *Their general turned the blockade to a play.*
> *Poor vain poltroons, with justice we'll retort,*
> *And call them blockheads for their idle sport.*

The New England militia army maintaining the land blockade of Boston now was joined by hundreds of volunteers marching in from other colonies, some from as far away as the backwoods of Virginia. For the first time, large numbers of men from different regions of America met and mingled.

One rebel wrote in his journal that it was fascinating how "people from distant colonies, differing in manners and prejudices, could at once harmonize in friendly intercourse. Hence we too frequently hear the burlesque epithet of Yankee from one party, and that of Buckskin, by way of retort, from another."

Relations were not always friendly, however. George Washington, who had his own problems managing the siege, building a reliable staff at the Cambridge headquarters, and dealing with serious supply and manpower shortages, sometimes had to step in and break up fist fights between men of different regions. Somehow he held his army together that precarious winter of 1775-76, even though word came of a New Year's Eve repulse at Quebec and the death of the fine commander, James Montgomery.

Spirits rose when a desperately needed supply of artillery arrived, transported from the captured forts on Lake Champlain. The guns had been laboriously brought overland through the snow by men led by General Henry Knox — a self-taught artilleryman and himself a Bostonian. In March, again working under cover of darkness, Washington's army dug artillery emplacements on Dorchester Heights and other positions commanding Boston. Now they had enough firepower to drive the British fleet from the harbor and batter Boston to rubble if they wished. Should the British try to root out this new threat, they would have to attack frontally. This time, unlike at Breed's Hill, the rebels had taken strong positions that offered little chance to outflank or cut them off.

Instead of shedding more soldier blood, however, the British abruptly abandoned the city. Soldiers and loyalists and their families crowded into ships of every size and shape and sailed away to Halifax, Nova Scotia. It was another astonishing achievement by the rebels, who paraded triumphantly into Boston to the tune of "Yankee Doodle."

Even after two bloody engagements and the evacuation of Boston, most loyalists considered rebel militias useless in battle unless they were dug in — as they had done years ago at Fortress Louisbourg, last year at Bunker Hill, and then with such success on Dorchester Heights. To stand up to British soldiers in the open field took courage the Yankee rebels did not have, said a loyalist poet in Halifax. The writer entitled the work "Burrowing Yankees."

> *Ye Yankees who, mole-like, still throw up the earth,*
> *And like them, to your follies are blind from your birth;*
> *Attempt not to hold British troops at defiance,*
> *True Britons with whom you pretend an alliance.*
> *And the time will soon come when your whole rebel race*

Evacuating Boston in March, 1776, the British and loyalists sail away for Halifax, Nova Scotia, never again to return.

Will be drove from the lands, nor dare show your face:
Here's health to great George, may he fully determine,
To root from the earth all such insolent vermin.

Later that spring of 1776, Washington heard the dismal news that the Quebec campaign had utterly failed, that the British in Canada had been reinforced by a fleet and a new army, and the Americans were retreating southward.

This war for control of the colonies was paralleled by a struggle for ownership of "Yankee Doodle." Throughout the Revolution, it was the British and loyalists who produced most of the insulting verses published in America and back in Britain. The loyalists at Quebec took their turn, too, and someone who had endured the siege there employed the "Yankee Doodle" tune for new verses.

Benedict Arnold, formerly a successful trader in horses and the leader of a little army that had pushed through the Maine wilderness to surprise the redcoats in Canada, was a worthy target for loyalist spite.

Arnold is as brave a man
As ever dealt in horses,
And now commands a numerous clan
Of New-England Jack-asses.

Entitled "A New Song," and first published in an English newspaper, this piece mocks the prominent revolutionary officers by name, calling them nothing more than tradesmen, black-smiths, and butchers aspiring to be officers. It is one of the first occasions in print where all rebel Americans are lumped under the term "Yankey."

> *'Tis thus, my friends, we are beset,*
> *By all those d—n'd invaders;*
> *No greater villains ever met,*
> *Than are those Yankey leaders.*

The rebels kept their own verses coming, too. An old stanza that praised one town over another had changed along the way, recalling the destruction of Charlestown during the Battle of Bunker Hill.

> *Marblehead's a rocky place,*
> *Cape Cod is sandy,*
> *Charles Town is burnt down,*
> *Boston is the dandy!*

And the racy verses were always fun.

> *Pumpkin pie is very good*
> *And so is apple lantern,*
> *Had you been whipped as oft as I,*
> *You'd not have been so wanton.*

Young Harvard graduate Edward Bangs visited his family home on Cape Cod and there wrote down some of the "Yankey

Song" verses he had heard around the American camp at Cambridge. Bangs was known to "have a taste for poetry," according to contemporaries, and some of his compositions were published widely in various journals: "His odes for public festive occasions were of respectable merit."

Friends of Bangs knew he had written down verses to "The Yankey Song," and some thought he had actually composed them himself. In time, others would have the misconception that the "Visit to Camp" motifs of the "Yankey Song" were his alone.

I n July, 1776, the Continental Congress in Philadelphia declared independence from Britain. In this time a light dragoon regiment rode down from Connecticut to Philadelphia, attracting attention and admiration because many of them, quite elderly, proudly wore their uniforms from the 1745 Louisbourg campaign. "Some of them assisted, in the present uniforms, at the first reduction of Louisbourg, and their lank, lean cheeks and war-worn coats are viewed with… veneration…." said a local newspaper. The sophisticates of cosmopolitan Philadelphia — the second-largest city in the British empire after London — were delighted with these gray-haired Yankee dragoons, calling them true "irregulars…so little were they like modern soldiers in air or costume."

"Yankee Doodle" and the term "Yankee" already had become widely known throughout the states and to the British as symbols of American resistance.

That summer of 1776, a royal fleet under Sir Peter Parker was repulsed attempting to capture Sullivan's Island near Charleston, South Carolina. Later, a rebel wrote a song about the battle, pretending the composer was Sir Peter, himself, who laments the damage to his flagship, HMS *Bristol*. Entitled "A New War Song by Sir Peter Parker," it is set to the tune "Well Met Brother Tar."

> *With much labor and toil,*
> *Unto Sullivan's Isle,*
> *I came firm as Falstaff or Pistol,*
> *But the Yankees, God rot 'em,*
> *I could not get at 'em,*
> *Most terribly mauled my poor* Bristol.

Defeated, and with much loss, Parker sails away from Charleston, and as he goes, he refers sidelong to a near-miss during the fighting, which wounded his leg and tore off his breeches so that:

> *I've the wind in my tail,*
> *And I'm hoisting my sail,*
> *To leave Sullivan's Island behind me.*

The admiral predicts that even though he could not capture this small island, the British will take the whole continent within a year: "If the cowardly Yankees will let us." Parker was repulsed by Southern rebels for the most part, not New England Yankees, but the writer of the song plays on the stereotypical

British ignorance of Americans, calling them all Yankees and, as usual, cowards.

Although Charleston was a rebel triumph, a series of disasters befell Washington and his little army in this period. Howe defeated him on Long Island and captured New York City, which became the stronghold of redcoats and loyalists for the rest of the war. New York was the home of loyalist publisher James Rivington, who enthusiastically printed songs insulting the rebels. John Vardill, the clever 1770 loyalist versifier who had mocked Isaac Sears with "The Procession," had nothing more to offer, however, having fled New York and the wrath of the Liberty Boys before the war broke out. In England and France, Vardill served the royal government as one of its most brilliant espionage agents, intercepting messages to the Continental Congress from delegate Silas Deane in France.

Rivington had reason to hate revolutionaries, for in 1775 the Liberty Boys and Isaac Sears had gone on an anti-loyalist rampage in New York City and destroyed his newspaper print shop. Sears's Connecticut-based Liberty Boys reveled in "Yankee Doodle," and once tormented a loyalist by standing him in a large hogshead and making him sing and dance to the tune all night long. Had they caught Rivington, the loyalist mouthpiece, they might have done much worse to him. His press criticized the rebels at every turn, and he had plenty to crow about in the second half of 1776, a time of rebel retreats — until Christmas, that is, when Washington defeated a force of Hessians at Trenton, New Jersey, an inspiring triumph immediately followed

by another at Princeton early in January 1777. In March, short-
ly after Washington's surprising victories, the "Song of the
Minute Man" was written at Boundbrook, in central New Jersey.
Sung to the tune of "The Girl I Left Behind Me," it is unkind
to stay-at-home patriots and takes fierce pride in the name
Minute Man. This song exemplifies how eagerly "Yankee
Doodle" had been adopted by other colonies; it warns patriots
not to be dismayed if the "Tories thunder," because:

> *If they advance,*
> *We will make them dance*
> *The tune of Yankee Doodle.*

The first great success of the combined forces of the former colonies came late in 1777, and at the expense of
General Burgoyne, who had been given command of a
splendid army of British, Brunswick Germans, loyalists, and
Indians. Burgoyne invaded down the Lake Champlain–Hudson
River corridor toward Albany, where he expected to meet a
smaller royal force advancing from the west and a British attack
northward from New York City.

At first, it appeared the rebel Northern Army under Philip
Schuyler was doomed to defeat. Schuyler organized a fighting
withdrawal against Burgoyne's powerful army, which forced the
rebels to abandon forts at Crown Point and Ticonderoga.
Yankee troops stubbornly engaged a British and German recon-
naissance in force at Hubbardton (now in Vermont), and

Schuyler sent forward Dutch Yorkers and New England troops who blunted the British vanguard in the woods near Fort Anne. As Burgoyne hesitated, deciding his next move, Schuyler had his own men pitch into the forest and swamps, felling trees, diverting streams, and destroying scores of bridges to block Burgoyne's path to the Hudson.

In the tradition of their Dutch forebears, who had flooded the lands around Amsterdam to stop French invaders, these Yorkers from the Hudson Valley, New York City, and Long Island made more than twenty miles of woods impassable, delaying Burgoyne for weeks. Then Benedict Arnold was on the scene and, with Schuyler's cooperation, seemed everywhere at once — organizing militia reinforcements, leading Continental regulars to turn back the enemy's western force, and appearing in the nick of time at Saratoga to take the troops into battle. Thanks to Arnold's tactical genius, and despite the overly cautious rebel field commander General Horatio Gates (a native Englishman and the former captain of Richard Shuckburgh's Independent Company), Burgoyne was stopped cold at Saratoga.

By October, Burgoyne's army found itself surrounded, decimated, and starving, mainly the result of close cooperation between Yankee Arnold and Yorker Schuyler. On the British side, poor communication at the highest levels of command was the reason no strong force was sent from New York City to join the northern royal army. Burgoyne knew all hope was lost. His desperate troops begged for one last attempt at a breakout by making an almost suicidal attack, but Burgoyne wanted no such further sacrifice. He accepted surrender terms that gave his men full honors of war.

As his heartsick, angry soldiers cleaned their weapons and uniforms in preparation for the final ceremonies, they heard in the distance the sound of American fifes playing "Yankee Doodle." The victors were forming up in rank along the road for the vanquished to march through after grounding arms. If the rebels taunted them with that tune, then the battle could start all over again. So bitterly humiliated were the royal troops that one of the terms of surrender generously permitted them to ground arms in a secluded place, out of sight of the Americans. British armies simply did not surrender wholesale like this, especially not to ragtag amateurs.

When the time came to march down that road lined with thousands of enemy soldiers, however, Burgoyne's men could not avoid being much impressed by the fine discipline and smart turnout of the Americans, their banners and flags held proudly, but their fifes silent. As the survivors of regiment after regiment trudged past, the Americans stood at attention, respectful and solemn and soldierly, though the greatest pride and joy surged in their hearts.

A British officer later wrote: "I never shall forget the appearance of their troops on our marching past them; a dead silence universally reigned through their numerous columns, and even they seemed struck with our situation and dare scarce lift up their eyes to view British troops in such a situation. I must say

In the first great triumph of American arms, Burgoyne, left, surrenders his army to Gates, center, at Saratoga in northern New York, in October 1777.

their decent behaviour during the time (to us so greatly fallen) merited the utmost approbation and praise."

No one played "Yankee Doodle."

Saratoga was the turning point of the American Revolution, winning the the former colonies the open support of France, which eventually entered the war on their side. Now, the name "Yankee" appeared in many a war song, and was always a point of pride to the rebels, whether they were New Englanders or not. John Paul Jones, the outstanding American naval hero, was a Scotsman by birth, but when he raided the British coast in the spring of 1778, a song in his praise was entitled "The Yankee Man-of-War." A year later, his *Bonhomme Richard* defeated the *Serapis,* a famous triumph commemorated in the song "Paul Jones's Victory." Originally an English composition that later became popular in America, it gives Jones a ringing declamation in the heat of battle:

> *"We'll receive a broadside from this bold Englishman,*
> *And like true Yankee sailors return it again."*

Other popular war songs included the name "Yankee" in ways that often could never have been imagined in the era before the Revolution, both favorably and unfavorably. In "The Saratoga Song":

> *The British fought like lions,*
> *And we like Yankees bold.*

In one anti-Revolutionary song Yankees were equated with Frenchmen and Spaniards, traditionally British enemies. Another pro-British song, "The Rebels," was written by a loyalist ranger officer who apparently was not at Saratoga to see the impressive carriage of the Americans at the surrender:

> Come listen awhile, and I'll sing you a song;
> I'll show you those Yankees are all in the wrong,
> Who, with blustering look and most awkward gait,
> 'Gainst their lawful sovereign dare for to prate.

Early in 1778, loyalist publisher Rivington had the challenging task of outdoing a rebel song about a quirky non-battle that had taken place in the Delaware River that winter. Written by patriot Francis Hopkinson, "The Battle of the Kegs" became a favorite of the rebels. It is set to the tune of "Yankee Doodle" and tells about some incendiary devices, "infernals," created by Connecticut inventor David Bushnell, who later would build the first submarine. Bushnell devised floating mines out of powder kegs and sent them down the Delaware, intending to wreak havoc with British shipping at Philadelphia.

Alert British sailors and soldiers took up positions wherever they could to fire desperately at the mines and blow them up before they struck a vessel. In the end, little damage was done, but Bushnell's novel scheme inspired Hopkinson to laugh at king's fighting men trying frantically to sink some wooden kegs. A verse has Sir Henry Clinton, the notoriously lethargic British commander, trundling out of a warm bed upon hearing the alarm and reluctantly leaving his mistress, the wife of an ambitious commissary officer. Sir Henry resolutely sets all his forces into motion to do battle.

> *"Therefore prepare for bloody war;*
> *These kegs must all be routed,*
> *Or surely we despised shall be,*
> *And British courage doubted."*

> *The royal band now ready stand,*
> *All ranged in dread array, sir,*
> *With stomach stout, to see it out,*
> *And make a bloody day, sir.*

> *Such feats did they perform that day*
> *Against those wicked kegs, sir,*
> *That years to come, if they get home,*
> *They'll make their boasts and brags, sir.*

There also appeared in print that year one of Rivington's best attempts to parody American rebel fighting abilities. Also to the tune of "Yankee Doodle," it scoffed at a failed Franco-American expedition to Rhode Island in August. After a brief engagement with the British fleet, French admiral d'Estaing sailed away, leaving the rebels to fend for themselves against superior enemy land forces. Entitled "Yankee Doodle's Expedition to Rhode Island," the ballad tells how Brother Jonathan had felt so very bold, believing he had the support of the powerful French.

So Yankee Doodle did forget
The sound of British drum, sir,
How oft it made him quake and sweat,
In spite of Yankee rum, sir.

As Jonathan so much desir'd
To shine in martial story,
D'Estaing with politesse retir'd,
To leave him all the glory.

French artillery firing from the allies' siege works at Yorktown in 1781, as Washington, center, looks toward the defenses of Cornwallis's trapped army.

Another dart from Rivington's press was "A New Song," in 1779, commemorating the British capture of Savannah and described by the publisher as "a new song to an old tune, written by a Yankee and sung to the tune of Doodle doo." Again, the French are accused of failing the Americans.

> *The Frenchmen came upon the coast,*
> *Our great allies, and they did boast,*
> *They soon would bang the British host,*
> *Doodle doodle doo,*
> *Pa, pa, pa, pa, pa.*

> *But soon we found ourselves mistaken,*
> *And we were glad to save our bacon,*
> *Rather than be killed or taken,*
> *Doodle doodle doo,*
> *Pa, pa, pa, pa, pa.*

The British found another way to turn "Yankee Doodle" into an insult: their bands often played it within hearing of the American lines, and at just the right moment they added "raspberries" — insulting, rude sounds. This instrumental trick was imitated by the Americans, who would play some hallowed British favorite, such as "God Save the King," with a raspberry of their own. So frequent and common was this insult that commanders involved in arranging delicate surrender ceremonies were obliged to require that neither victor nor vanquished be allowed to play any of the other side's tunes, lest the musical insults get out of hand and a brawl begin.

The most memorable surrender of all the Revolution took place on October 19, 1781, when a British army led by General Lord Cornwallis capitulated at Yorktown, Virginia, to the combined forces of Washington and the French allies. This last major campaign of the war ended exactly four years after Burgoyne's decisive defeat at Saratoga.

For the surrender ceremony, the Americans stood in ranks on one side of the road, facing the ranks of the French army, together forming a long corridor from the British lines to the place of grounding arms. As at Saratoga, the Americans were requested by their commanders to be respectfully silent as the British marched through, and they were. The half-intoxicated French, however, especially the preened and gorgeous young officers, could not contain their elation at seeing their old enemies laid low, and many laughed aloud at the British. For all the soldierly bearing of the Americans, and despite the French grins, the sullen redcoats striding between their ranks kept their heads rigidly turned toward the French, bluntly ignoring the Continental Army.

It was as crude an insult as any Britisher could hurl at the Americans, and Washington's young French aide, the Marquis de Lafayette, bridled. Furious, Lafayette snapped out a command to nearby American musicians. Fifes and drums exploded with a racket that startled the British, who jerked their heads

A French painting depicts the surrender of Cornwallis to Washington at Yorktown; American and French troops form a corridor through which the British Army marches on its way to grounding arms.

around as one man, unintentionally acknowledging the triumphant Americans, whose resounding music was "Yankee Doodle."

Thus was the last act of the Revolutionary War played out to America's song of triumph and liberty.

> *Let tyrants shake their iron rod,*
> *And slavery clank her galling chains;*
> *We fear them not; we trust in God —*
> *New England's God for ever reigns.*

From "Chester," a hymn composed in 1778 by William Billings, born in Boston in 1746; this was the most popular song of the New England soldiers, who sang several patriotic Billings tunes, often teaching them to people in the states where they campaigned.

Seven

AMERICA'S SONG

Yankee Doodle, guard your coast,
Yankee Doodle dandy,
Fear not, then, nor threat nor boast,
Yankee Doodle dandy.

From "The New Yankee Doodle," a 1798 song that called on
Americans to prepare for a possible war with France.

I N 1783, PEACE WAS MADE, the American Revolution won,
and the thirteen states were free to shape their own future.
The next four years were a rough and uncertain journey
from making a war to making a union, on a path strewn with
regional jealousies and bitter dissension. As America endured
the confederation crisis, there was always the lurking threat of
attack from foreign powers.

If Americans did not yet know who they were as a nation, they did know who they were as citizens of their own independent state or as the inheritors of the torch passed on from the first colonists, whether Virginians, Yorkers, or New Englanders. The British and French may have considered all Americans as Yankees, but in the new states there was a clear understanding that Yankee Jonathan was a stereotypical rustic from New England, talkative, full of humor, and quick to fight if he thought his independence was threatened.

The first real portrayal of the stage Yankee appeared in *The Contrast,* a comedy performed in 1787 in New York City. Written by Boston native and Harvard graduate Royall Tyler, this was the first American play performed in public by a company of professional actors. Tyler had served as an officer during the Revolution, and he well knew both the song "Yankee Doodle" and the Yankee soldier. His play humorously depicts the "contrast" between the simple honesty of idealized American society and the hypocrisy of fashionable culture that was corrupting that society.

Tyler's naive, homespun Jonathan from the Massachusetts back country is bursting with the enthusiasm of the lusty country boy who has just won a war, has a heart of gold, but also a fiery temper. Evoking a sense of patriotism while joshing rebel hero and social climber alike, *The Contrast* was a great public success thanks in part to the charm and broad appeal of Yankee Jonathan. The comedy sparked yet another revolution in America: a new and sudden love of the theater. For the first time drama and the theater were opened up to all the American people, even to the once-hostile New Englanders.

The Contrast's prologue wastes no time in getting to the point, and in the very first line stirs up American emotions still heated from years of war. A "Gentleman from New York" addresses the audience:

> *Exult, each patriot heart! — this night is shown*
> *A piece, which we may fairly call our own;*
> *Where the proud titles of "My Lord! Your Grace!"*
> *To humble Mister and plain Sir give place.*
> *Our Author pictures not from foreign climes*
> *The fashions or the follies of the times;*
> *But has confin'd the subject of his work*
> *To the gay scenes — the circles of New-York.*

The narrator calls on Americans not to "ape the rich or great," but to prize virtue and the "solid good."

> *But modern youths, with imitative sense,*
> *Deem taste in dress the proof of excellence;*
> *And spurn the meanness of your homespun arts,*
> *Since homespun habits would obscure their parts;*
> *Whilst all, which aims at splendour and parade,*
> *Must come from Europe, and be ready made.*
> *Strange! We should thus our native worth disclaim,*
> *And check the progress of our rising fame.*

In a subplot to the main romance between a dashing Yankee colonel and a New York City maiden of virtue, Jonathan becomes mixed up with high society, including the pretty Jenny, a serving girl. Her conniving suitor, Jessamy, also a servant, has persuaded Jonathan that it would be good citified form to give Jenny a kiss the very first chance he got. Jessamy hopes the sharp "contrast" between his own fashionable, delicate manners and Jonathan's clumsy, "nauseous pawings" will make Jenny hasten into Jessamy's arms.

Jonathan tells Jenny of the strange things and people he has seen in New York, saying he had unknowingly entered some private home and was dismayed by all the shocking goings-on there. Then, when he tried to get out of the place someone demanded that he pay for having been there. When Jonathan asked why he had to pay, the fellow told him he had been watching the "School for Scandal." Jonathan responds:

> JONATHAN: The School for Scandalization! — Oh! ho! no wonder you New-York folks are so 'cute at it, when you go to school to learn it....

Jenny realizes he had gone into the theater, and when she sees he is so upset talking about the confusing sights of New York, she asks him to sing a song for her instead. He knows only hymns, he replies.

> JONATHAN: Why, all my tunes're go-to-meeting tunes, save one, and I count you won't altogether like that 'ere.
>
> JENNY: What is it called?

JONATHAN: I am sure you have heard folks talk about it; it is called "Yankee Doodle."

At Jenny's insistence, Jonathan sings, including the verse about going to militia camp with Father and then two more about the "swamping gun" and firing it off. He begins a third verse, but stops short because it was about to be vulgar and would embarrass Jenny.

She asks if there are no other verses to the song:

JONATHAN: No, no; I can sing more; some other time, when you and I are better acquainted, I'll sing the whole of it — no, no — that's a fib — I can't sing but a hundred and ninety verses; our Tabitha at home can sing it all. — [Sings.]

> Marblehead's a rocky place,
> And Cape-Cod is sandy;
> Charlestown is burnt down,
> Boston is the dandy.
> Yankee doodle, doodle doo, etc.

I vow, my own town song has put me into such topping spirits that I believe I'll begin to do a little, as Jessamy says we must when we go a-courting. — [Runs and kisses her.] Burning rivers! Cooling flames! Red-hot roses! Pig-nuts! Hasty-pudding and ambrosia!

Jenny slaps his face for his audacity, and when he proposes marriage she exits in a fury. The Yankee colonel will win the hand of his own dearest, but Yankee Jonathan does not like being slapped when he thought Jenny really wanted a kiss. He longs to go home.

> JONATHAN: If this is the way with your city ladies, give me the twenty acres of rock, the Bible, the cow, and Tabitha, and a little peaceable bundling.

During those first years after the Revolution, debate raged over how to join the thirteen independent states into a federation, create a federal government and constitution, and at the same time guarantee fundamental rights for the people.

Soon after ratifying the proposed Bill of Rights, the pro-Federalist party in Massachusetts used the tune of "Yankee Doodle" for verses that encouraged national unity. Called "A Yankee Federal Song," it also held up New England as an example of how to overcome political differences by discussing issues in an honest spirit of openness. Their song is about Yankees holding their Bill of Rights ratification convention in Boston as if it were a local town meeting.

The song tells that after windy speeches by John Hancock, "who dearly loves the nation," they reached a "concil'atory plan" that "prevented much vexation," and at last compromised for the sake of the common good and future prosperity:

> *The question being outright put,*
> *(Each voter independent),*

> *The Fed'ralists agreed t'adopt,*
> *And then propose amendment.*

The voting done, the delegates set aside their differences, and everyone "went to dine, sir."

> *Oh, then a whapping feast began,*
> *And all hands went to eating;*
> *They drank their toasts, shook hands and sang,*
> *Huzza! for 'vention meeting!*

> *Now politicians of all kinds*
> *Who are not yet decided,*
> *May see how Yankees speak their minds*
> *And yet are not divided.*

> *So here I end my Fed'ral song,*
> *Composed of thirteen verses;*
> *May agriculture flourish long,*
> *And commerce fill our purses.*

The melody and spirit of "Yankee Doodle" became known around the young nation and the world, adapted again and again with new verses that suited the purpose and the moment. The Federalist party used the tune for its own anthem, and in 1795 an orchestral adaptation was part of the "Federal Overture," composed by Benjamin Carr to celebrate the unity of the new United States. The British still used the melody for various anti-American verses, and it is said that French revolutionaries sometimes played it as a marching song early in their 1789 uprising.

A decade later, relations with revolutionary France had deteriorated, for the United States was caught between the combatants of the Napoleonic Wars. The Americans were rising in power and prestige as merchant seamen, but British blockades of France and French blockades of Britain put American sailors in peril of being attacked by both.

In 1798, when "The New Yankee Doodle" appeared, France was the most likely next enemy of "Columbia," as America was sometimes called.

> *Columbians all, the present hour*
> *As Brothers should unite us.*
> *Union at home's the only way*
> *To make each nation right us.*
>
> *Yankee Doodle, guard your coast*
> *Yankee Doodle dandy*
> *Fear not, then, nor threat nor boast,*
> *Yankee Doodle dandy.*

War with France was averted, but Anglo-American affairs worsened, and in the summer of 1812 matters came to a head. The United States declared war on Great Britain, which had blockaded the Continent and was boarding American ships both to look for contraband and to force British-born sailors into the Royal Navy.

That August, the USS *Constitution*, commanded by Isaac Hull, defeated the HMS *Guerriere*, under James Dacres. Seafaring New England was especially thrilled by the victory, and an anonymous Yankee adapted the popular sailor song "Brandy-O" to commemorate the fight. Entitled "The Constitution and the Guerriere" — sometimes also called "Yankee Doodle Dandy-O" — the song glories in the rising reputation of the Yankee seaman.

> *It oft-times has been told*
> *That the British seamen bold*
> *Could flog the tars of France*
> *So neat and handy-O!*
> *But they never found their match*
> *Till the Yankees did them catch,*
> *Oh, the Yankee boys for fighting are the dandy-O!*

According to the song, the Americans pour their first broadside into the *Guerriere*, carrying away the mainmast and dismaying Captain Dacres, who groans, "I didn't think those Yankees were so handy-O!"

> *Our second told so well*
> *That their fore and mizzen fell,*
> *Which doused the royal ensign neat and handy-O!*

> *"By George," says he, "we're done,"*
> *And they fired a lee gun,*
> *While the Yankees struck up Yankee Doodle Dandy-O!*

It was turnabout a year later, when HMS *Shannon* captured the USS *Chesapeake* in a brief but savage battle. The dying American commander, James Lawrence, exhorted his men to fight on with the famous last words, "Don't give up the ship!" The British sailors later took the opportunity to mock the Yankees, using the same tune, "Brandy-O," in their own song, "The Shannon and the Chesapeake."

> *Now the* Chesapeake *so bold,*
> *Out of Boston, we've been told,*
> *Came to take the British frigate neat and handy-O!*
> *All the people of the port,*
> *They came out to see the sport,*
> *And the bands were playing Yankee Doodle Dandy-O!*

The fight lasted only twenty minutes, and the Shannon's Captain Philip Broke led his men to victory, though he was seriously wounded.

> *We no sooner had begun*
> *Than from their guns they run,*
> *Though before they thought they worked 'em neat*
> * and handy-O!*
> *Brave Broke, he waved his sword,*

Crying, "Now, my lads, we'll board,
And we'll stop their playing Yankee Doodle Dandy-O!"

Fighting Yankees on land and sea was the subject of several British songs during the War of 1812, in which the United States was overmatched for the most part. One song, "Come All You Bold Canadians," called on men to muster to "fight those proud Yankees" who attempted several unsuccessful invasions of Canada. The worst American land defeat was the humiliating surrender of Detroit in the summer of 1812 to a force of British regulars, Canadians, and Indians. Detroit's commander was General William Hull, a Connecticut man who had fought with distinction in the Revolution but surrendered without a fight, reputedly fearing an Indian massacre. Having brought down accusations of cowardice on his head, Hull also inspired the Canadians to rework old verses of the original "Yankee Doodle."

Brother Ephraim, he's come back
Proved an arrant coward,
Afraid to fight the enemy,
Afeared he'd be devoured.

The War of 1812 gave birth to the figure of "Uncle Sam," the whipcord tough, but good-natured character with the self-righteous determination of Yankee Jonathan. Uncle Sam sprang into the popular mind as the symbol of the newly forged, unified American nation, and in time replaced Yankee Jonathan as the representation of the United States.

After 1800, the term "Yankee" became proudly joined to "seaman" as American sailors and ships became second to none, as proven by the stunning victory of

the USS Constitution *over HMS* Guerriere *in the War of 1812 —
an engagement celebrated in a popular song praising "Yankee boys."*

Much of this war's conflict was on the high seas, and thousands of American sailors were captured, many confined to bleak, crowded Dartmoor Prison in England. Yet even in captivity, they found a way to defy the British: on Washington's birthday, February 22, 1815, the American prisoners assembled a marching band of fifes, flutes, bugles, trumpets, clarinets, and even violins to play a rousing "Yankee Doodle," much to the annoyance of high-ranking British officers who were visiting the prison.

"Yankee Doodle" was not only a song of American defiance, but in one instance just the playing of the tune was enough to repel a British attack. This happened in the fall of 1814 at the harbor town of Scituate, Massachusetts, when the British warship *La Hogue* appeared offshore and sent a boat full of men toward land. No American fighting force was on hand to prevent the enemy from seizing laden vessels tied up at the town wharf and perhaps setting fire to the place. There were, however, the two Bates sisters — Abigail, fifteen, and Rebecca, sixteen — who were at home by themselves when they first saw the boat pulling for shore.

The girls made up their minds to do something rather than just watch a raid that might end with their own home in ruins. Their father's fife and drum from the Revolution hung in places of honor on the wall, so Rebecca grabbed the fife and Abigail strapped on the drum. Off they hurried to the lighthouse and hid behind a shed as the British boat entered the undefended harbor. Suddenly, Rebecca shrilled out "Yankee Doodle" on the fife, and Abigail beat the drum as hard as she could. The racket carried over the water, sounding like a call to arms, and even the captain aboard the *La Hogue* heard it.

The oarsmen in the boat hesitated, looking for some sign of the militia mustering to oppose them. Their captain aboard ship decided things for them and fired a signal gun, calling the invaders to turn back, which they hurriedly did. Rebecca and Abigail Bates and "Yankee Doodle" saved Scituate that day.

The greatest American victory of the War of 1812 was the Battle of New Orleans, fought on January 8, 1815, after the British fleet and an army of veteran redcoats had besieged the city through the autumn and early winter. The British methodically prepared to storm New Orleans, moving their lines steadily closer to the defensive works commanded by Andrew Jackson, who led fighting men mainly from the Mississippi valley and its tributaries. During the period of siege, a young redcoat subaltern — the lowest ranking officer in the army — so enjoyed hearing the American bands play each morning just before dawn, that one night he crept across no-man's-land for a better listening post.

This fellow had to slip past his own picket guard to do it and risked discovery by sharpshooting Kentucky riflemen on sentry duty. Lying there in the predawn darkness, he listened as musicians from the Appalachian Mountains and the Mississippi valley played familiar old tunes in their uniquely American style. Some melodies he had never heard before, and it was a fascinating and moving experience when some "waltzes struck me as

Old soldiers on Independence Day: during the nineteenth century, the favorite patriotic march to the sound of fife and drum was always "Yankee Doodle."

being peculiarly beautiful." Apparently, he thought those lovely waltzes worth imperiling his life to hear, but he complained that between them he had to listen to "Yankee Doodle" at least six times.

On January 8, 1815, the British Army facing New Orleans once again displayed misbegotten arrogance when fighting Americans and made frontal assaults against Jackson's defenses. The seventy-five hundred redcoat attackers were repulsed, suffering more than two thousand killed and wounded, a slaughter reminiscent of Breed's Hill forty years earlier. Only a handful of Americans were casualties. The British immediately packed up and sailed away from New Orleans, defeated, unaware that two weeks earlier a peace treaty had been signed at Ghent in Belgium.

Just before the banquet to celebrate the signing of the Treaty of Ghent on January 5, the Belgian orchestra director asked American dignitaries — including the likes of Massachusetts Yankee John Adams, and Virginian Henry Clay — which of their national airs they wanted played for the occasion.

"Hail, Columbia" and "Yankee Doodle" both were recommended, but the director did not know the music for "Yankee Doodle" so he asked them to sing or whistle it for him. None of these prominent Americans felt up to the task, claiming they could not carry a tune. Then Clay, the Southerner, had the answer, and he rang a bell to summon his black servant.

"John," Clay said, "whistle 'Yankee Doodle' for this gentleman."

The man did so, and the director wrote down the notes. At the banquet the orchestra performed the tune brilliantly, of course adding a few appealing variations of its own — as almost everyone down the centuries has done with "Yankee Doodle."

Yet, it was not the variety of verses or the delightful musical interpretations that made "Yankee Doodle" the best-loved song of America. It is the national memory that "Yankee Doodle" calls up, the memory of a people fighting for freedom against all the odds, risking everything and, in the end, winning their liberty — liberty that ever and again must be defended and shared and sung about.

For America's Song is a song of liberty.

> *Yankee Doodle keep it up,*
> *Yankee Doodle Dandy!*

THE END

PART II

The Study

MUSICOLOGY,
ETYMOLOGY, AND MYTH

WHERE DOES AN ANCIENT MELODY COME FROM? Where does "Yankee Doodle" come from — the song as well as the name? After the American Revolution and throughout the nineteenth century, scholars chased the answers to these questions and found bits and pieces of evidence, but for all their efforts, no one put everything together into a coherent explanation.

In part, this was because the history-writing Americans of the nineteenth century did not understand the importance of the colonial Dutch to the foundations of American culture, nor did they realize the bitterness and hostility between New Netherlanders and New Englanders in the 1600s. A diluted version of that hostility was transferred to the first English New Yorkers, mainly royalists who had fought a long and ferocious civil war against the European cousins (and siblings and parents) of Puritan New Englanders.

Hard feelings were mutual between Yorkers — Dutch colonists or English colonists — and the New Englanders they called Jankes, later Yankees, and sometimes Janke Doodles. If the depth of hostility between Yorkers and Yankees is not taken into account — as the great musicologist Oscar Sonneck did not do in his otherwise beautifully realized 1909 Library of Congress report on "Yankee Doodle" — then the original power of Yankee and Doodle cannot be comprehended. Anyone who looks objectively into the forty years of early Dutch settlement and the subsequent century of pervasive Dutch influence in so many aspects of America's development will come to understand how much has been neglected by historians.

Even today, in parts of Holland, the term "Janikens," one form of Janke, still carries with it the lingering sense of indicating a religious group of some sort, as if remembering the English Separatists who had come to live among them in the early 1600s.

Is the harvest song of Chapter One a definite early version of Janke Doedel? Likely not, but it could be, and the words used here are slightly different from those the scholars recorded around 1855, the height of enthusiasm for research into "Yankee Doodle." These are not all nonsense words, for *landheer*, like *jonker*, means lord of the land. Was the jonker, or sometimes *jonkheer*, really sung about as a doodle, or fool? He could have been, and this silly jonker might not have been able to see the town for the houses. Thus does a folk song evolve.

The same later with the harvest song verses in English: these may have come to be many years later than 1664, but in this chapter they represent the sort of verses that might have been sung to the tune we know as "Yankee Doodle," and which in the mid-1600s was more likely known as the "doodle-doo" tune. These versions might not be historically confirmable, but they capture the spirit of the time and of the song that was carrying forward the air that one day became "Yankee Doodle." Of course, there is evidence in military fife books of the later eighteenth century that a number of tunes were called "Yankee Doodle" or "Yankee Tootle." An educated guess is that the one we know best was the one actually considered to be the "Yankee song," a New England folk air that people tootled on flutes and danced to.

In his report on "Yankee Doodle," Sonneck pulled apart the oft-mentioned notion that the royalist Cavaliers of the English Civil War sang the following to mock Oliver Cromwell, the leader of the Puritans fighting the royalists.

> *Nankee Doodle came to town*
> *Upon a Kentish pony.*
> *He stuck a feather in his hat*
> *And called him Macaroni.*

In this nineteenth-century engraving, Massachusetts militiamen play "Yankee Doodle" on rebel earthworks at Breed's Hill on the morning of June 17, 1775.

Quoting the expert British ballad authority, Rev. T. Woodfall Ebsworth, Sonneck asserted that there simply was no such song, which some supposedly called "The Roundheads and the Cavaliers." Others disagreed and said anecdotal evidence indicates such a ditty really was sung, and still others that the Puritans sang a comparable ditty that made fun of Prince Rupert, the best royalist commander of the war. None says what a "Nankee" is.

SONNECK QUOTED FROM THE AMERICAN EDUCATOR and historian George Ticknor's biography, in which it is said that Augustin Thierry, the French historian, believed Janke and Yankee originated from the "collision and jeerings" of the New Netherlanders and New Englanders. Sonneck did not accept this and went so far as to question whether the Dutch even used the name Janke, or Jancke. He wrote (in German) to a Dutch professor at the University of Leyden and received an answer in the affirmative, but he could just as well have spoken with Dutch Americans living in New York. He never fully accepted Janke as Yankee, although he reported that someone in 1760 had indeed described a ship as a "Dutch yanky."

Sonneck conceded that there is "a Dutch word which is almost identical with 'yankee,' but what sense can there possibly be in the combination of a Dutch ship with the word doodle, which means fool?…"

If "yanky" had been properly written in the text Sonneck saw, it would have been Janke, or Jantje, another Dutch diminutive for Jan, and it would have been understood as an English term for both a Dutch sailor or a Dutch sailing vessel. In seas where there was fighting between seafarers of England and Holland, Janke meant pirate to the English, though Janke might have considered himself a legitimate privateer, authorized by his government to prey on English ships.

So Sonneck came out against the likelihood that any colonial conflict between New Netherlanders and New Englanders could possibly have been so bitter as to produce the acrimony associated with "Yankee Doodle." He was objective, however, and included a report on scholar George H. Moore's paper entitled "On the Origin and History of Yankee Doodle," which Moore delivered in 1885 to the New York Historical Society. The report, published the next year in the *Magazine of American History*, said of Moore: "His theory of its derivation assigns the origin of the word to a Low-Dutch word janker, which signifies 'a howling cur, a yelper, a growler, a grumbling person,' and he formed the history of relations existing between the English and Dutch as sufficient reason for calling the English dogs."

Sonneck did not accept it that there were such hard feelings between Dutch and English colonials: he said Moore was "driving home the point with a vengeance." Of all the speculation on where "Yankee Doodle" came from, Sonneck decisively dismissed every one but the Dutch, about which he shrugged: "If the Dutch, on the other hand, do use Jancke (pronounced Yankee) in the sense of little John or Johnnie, then this would be the most plausible derivation, and 'Yankee Doodle' would be 'Johnny Doodle.'"

And if there were such deep-seated animosity between those colonies, then Yankee Doodle would understandably be a most infuriating insult to New Englanders. Which it certainly was.

Sonneck ended his wonderful report with this assessment: "The origin of 'Yankee Doodle' remains as mysterious as ever, unless it be deemed a positive result to have eliminated definitely almost every theory thus far advanced and thus by the process of elimination to have paved the way for an eventual solution of the puzzle."

THERE WERE STRONG CULTURAL AND LINGUISTIC ties between the Dutch and the English in the 1600s, whether they were at war with each other or at peace. (The first English governors of New England, and later of New York, virtually all spoke Dutch fluently.) In the United States, little is known about the Dutch who founded New

York and New Jersey and influenced the founding of several other states. One of the most telling shortcomings is the failure of literary surveys to include the three leading Dutch colonial poets who belong in any reputedly complete anthology of early American literature.

These are American colonists Hendricus Seylns, Nicasius de Sille, and Jacob Steendam, who loved America and whose fine writings have been translated into English but are virtually unknown, for all that they were notable adventurers, thinkers, and romantics in the spirit of the best of their time. Perhaps the most remarkable Dutch-American writer and adventurer was Adriaen van der Donck, who risked his life to speak out against the shortcomings of New Netherland and was exiled from his beloved New Amsterdam because he opposed the arbitrary tyranny of the Dutch West India Company. Van der Donck lost his battle with Pieter Stuyvesant and the Company, but he left as a legacy his *Description of New Netherland,* reminiscences of a lost home and an encouragement to Dutch folk to go and settle in America.

There was also the bold and brilliant Arent van Curler (or Corlear), founder of Schenectady, a fellow so fearless and so honest that the Indians loved him. Van Curler was a bit too daring, for while paddling with some Iroquois on a journey across Lake Champlain he laughed aloud when they warned him that they were passing a place of danger, where a demon lurked. Van Curler not only laughed, but he dropped his breeches and showed the demon his bare buttocks. A storm suddenly rose, and America lost one of its most adventurous early settlers. If the English did not, the Iroquois fondly remembered Corlear, and for another century referred to the successive governors of New York as "Corlear."

Little wonder that the Dutch-American origins of "Yankee Doodle" are not known if the likes of brash Corlear and lucid Van der Donck and the poets of New Netherland are not known either. American schoolchildren are even taught incorrectly that Peter Minuit, one of the early governors of New Netherland, bought Manhattan Island from the local Indians, when Minuit actually bought Staten Island because Manhattan had already been bought by his predecessor, Willem Verhulst.

New York scholar Alice P. Kenney wrote: "The history of New Netherland...is unfamiliar to Americans accustomed to think of colonial history in an English context."

Of course, it is not just the Dutch who have been almost invisible in the popular myth of colonial times — the Spanish, French, Africans, and others (women, too) — are also not seen enough, but they all are more visible in the colonial panorama than are the Dutch. When one studies "Yankee Doodle" in colonial times, however, the Dutch soon come to the fore.

STANDING ON THE SHOULDERS OF THE GIANT Oscar Sonneck and of those earlier scholars who searched so honestly for "Johnny Doodle," later researchers such as Lewis Maverick in 1962 and Leo LeMay in 1976 contributed to better understanding the mystery of "Yankee Doodle" 's origins.

Maverick, an economics professor, pulled together crucial evidence that Dr. Richard Shuckburgh was likely in the vicinity of Crailo and Albany and the Connecticut Yankee militiamen in 1755. He also proposed that the term "Yankee" could have come from the Cantonese shouting *yang kwei tzu* at British sailors in 1744. Maverick believed the sailors made their own pronunciation of this term — supposed to mean "ocean devil" or "foreign devil" — and theirs sounded more like "Yankee." These sailors then brought it back to England, where it was integrated into the vernacular, as were so many seafaring and nautical terms in those days.

Sonneck said that some have suggested "yankee" comes from a supposed Persian expression for a warlike man — *janghe* or *jenghe* (think Jenghis or Genghis Khan). In 1866, someone with only initials for identification wrote an article for a New England genealogical publication and said the Turks called America "Yankee Dooniah," meaning the "New World." Sonneck did not accept this one, either, as a key to the origin of Yankee Doodle.

Other theories claim the Indian peoples of the Hudson Valley and southwestward to the Delaware were first to call the New Englanders Yankees — supposedly their mispronunciation of the name English: the Delaware tribes' *Yengeesh* eventually became Yankees, it is said, and the rest is history. But the Dutch were trading with these peoples well before the Puritan Jankes showed up, and it is more likely that the Indians asked the Lowlanders who those other white folk were, and were told "Jankes," which the red folk pronounced Yengeesh. Then the white missionaries came among them and began to make a study of their languages and cultures while at the same time instilling the fear of the Christian god into them.

Rev. John Heckewelder, one of those itinerant missionaries, said in his early nineteenth-century writings that the Lenape of the Delaware River "exclusively applied" the name Yengees "to the people of New England, who, indeed, appear to have adopted it, and were, as they still are, generally throughout the country called Yankees, which is evidently the same name with a trifling alteration...."

Even back then, linguists were seeking the roots of Yankee, but Heckewelder does not seem fazed or confused by the fact that the Lenapes called all other English in America by the name "Saggenash," which sounds much like "Sassenach," the ancient Scottish and Irish term for those English Saxons they were always fighting. Why did the Lenni Lenape or Delawares not call all the Yengeesh in America Saggenash?

In his report, Sonneck made mincemeat of the Yengeesh theory of Yankee Doodle's nascency.

IN LEO LEMAY'S GUGGENHEIM FELLOWSHIP–fired search for the American origins of "Yankee Doodle," the Revolutionary War period was skillfully examined for evidence. An English professor, LeMay laid things out concisely and with magnificent footnoting that, taken alone, was worthy of a fellowship. He brought in the English folk song "Sir John Barleycorn" as the closest English "analogue for the Corn Stalks" refrain. He said "Sir John Barleycorn" was about the "planting, growing, harvesting, malting, and brewing of barley in terms of a magic and sacred death and resurrection. The American who wrote the Corn Stalks chorus may not have known any of its possible analogues, but the chorus is in the same mode as 'Sir John Barleycorn' — an uneasy combination of a burlesque tone with a sacred and cere-monial tone."

Where does an ancient melody come from? Where does it go?

It is interesting to realize that while John Barleycorn is the personi-fication of corn liquor, Jan Doedel is the Dutch name for a glass of gin.

The Corn Stalks refrain was still being sung in American variety shows on the nineteenth-century stage, with one version called "Corn Cobs Twist Your Hair Off" and sung to the tune of "Yankee Doodle." It employs old verses and new, one of which includes Davy Crockett of Indian wars and Alamo fame before the 1850s.

LeMay believed the corn stalks tune was originally danced to, and he added: "The Corn Stalk stanzas are folk songs, composed by differ-ent people on different occasions," and these "stanzas of indubitably American folk origin were evidently, like the Cape Breton group, in circulation by the 1740s." Not so fast, Mr. LeMay. He was right to make the assertion that the Cape Breton verses refer to the 1745 cam-paign, but there is no certainty that they were composed or known before 1755, when Dr. Shuckburgh could very well have written them at Fort Crailo in response to Yankee militiamen constantly boasting about their forefathers' achievements or else grumbling that Fortress

Louisbourg had unjustly been given back to the French by the damnable British government.

LeMay went on to say that the verses which make fun of bumpkin, rustic Yankees — in particular the lad who went up to camp with his father — were actually written by Americans as a hoax on the English. He said they could have been intended as "an ironic song written by a provincial about the splendid American victory" capturing Fortress Louisbourg. He considered the gentle joshing of the going-to-camp version not really harsh enough to be British redcoat mockery of Americans, and he added: "I think it is ironic. This ostensible satire of the provincial American militia is a perfect example of a dominant tradition of American humor. From the seventeenth century to the mid-twentieth, Americans have been keenly aware of English criticisms of their supposed barbarism. Colonial Americans learned to reply to English snobbery by deliberately posturing as unbelievably ignorant yokels. Thus, if the English believed the stereotype, they would be taken in by the Americans."

Very good. Except that the back-country Yankee militia who poured into Fort Crailo encampments during the French and Indian wars, poorly trained and scarcely equipped, really were ignorant yokels. The going-to-camp verses might seem to be just lighthearted teasing, but to New Englanders the Cape Breton campaign was no laughing matter. They surely did not find anything humorous in the home government nonchalantly returning the place in an exchange with the French. On top of that, the exchange benefited the politically powerful British West Indian planters, whose direct influence in Parliament brought on some of the most hated commercial restrictions against the American colonies and led to the conflict and unrest that resulted in the Revolution.

The Cape Breton stanzas were no joke to New Englanders, especially from out of the mouth of a British redcoat.

ONE OF THE EARLIEST USES OF "Yankee" among New Englanders was recalled in their old age by a pair of former Harvard students, who remembered a Cambridge farmer, Jonathan Hastings, being nicknamed "Yankey John" as far back as 1713. Hastings often used the term "yankey" when describing something as excellent — a "yankey" good horse, or "yankey" cider, and the Harvard blades of the day took to his style and used "yankey" the same way. Hastings was sometimes put forward as the first ever genuine Yankee — which is understandable considering the English-only prejudice to colonial history.

Yet the Scots used the word "yankie" in a similar vein, meaning "sharp, or clever," especially with regard to a woman. In old Scots, a "yanker" can be something done smartly, or it can mean a tall, agile, or clever girl, or an incessant talker. The Scottish use of "yanky" can signify nimble, active. Yankey Hastings rented horses to the students at Harvard, so he had reason to describe his stock as yankey good — nimble, active.

He did not, surely, also call them doodles.

The name "Yankee" was recorded in the 1725 inventory of a South Carolinian, whose possessions included "One negro man named Yankee to be sold." Likely this was originally the name Janke or Jan Kees, which the man had received because of Dutch influence. The Dutch were leading culprits in the slave trade, and in New Netherland there were many black "servants," as they were euphemistically called. Slaves in New Netherland were generally like lower-level members of the extended family, many of them permitted to earn their freedom in time, although their children — even if born after the parents had become free — usually were by law slaves from birth.

OF ALL THE SUSPECTS IN THE MYSTERY of Yankee Doodle, one of the most prime is the comic musical play, *The Beggar's Opera*, first performed in England in 1728. Written by John Gay, few cultural phenomena of the day short of all-out war had such a profound and jarring influence as did this riotous, knife-sharp ribald satire on English society as seen from the bottom up.

Set in the squalid underworld of criminal London, this ballad opera outrageously offered thieves and highwaymen as the main characters, and while not glamorizing or justifying their lives, it compared them on equal terms with the upper-class scoundrels who ran the government and pretended to be honorable men. Year after year for decades to come, *The Beggar's Opera* was performed somewhere in the British Empire, and even in Paris in 1750, about the same time it came to New York and the American colonies. Anyone in a position to attend the theater knew *The Beggar's Opera* with its sixty-nine songs, most made up of new and topical words put to popular old airs.

Maverick says one air was the original tune of "Yankee Doodle," but a study of the 1761 edition revealed no melodies that seemed to fit. Of course, as mentioned elsewhere, "Yankee Doodle" was sometimes a name given to tunes other than the one that became best known.

It might be that "Yankee Doodle" was the tune for one of the comic dance afterpieces that often accompanied American performances of *The Beggar's Opera.* An aspect of the genius and appeal of this ballad opera was that the performers added new material that would be appreciated by the particular audience in a particular place. It might well have been that one of the afterpieces, such as "The Drunken Peasant" or another described as "a clown dance," might have been to the tune otherwise known as "Yankee Doodle" or the "Yankey Song." If the actors, many of them visiting from England, wanted to delight a New York audience, they would have hit the mark by putting a doodle of a Yankee on stage.

It is noteworthy that the best-known performer of "The Drunken Peasant" was a gentleman billed as "Mr. Godwin," who was a professional dancing master well known in the South. It is noteworthy because of the "Captain Goodwin" or "Goodin" sung about with the men and boys at the militia camp. Was there an inside joke here? Were the Yankee men and boys supposedly trained by a famous dancing master best known for his clown dance or for "The Drunken Peasant"?

The Beggar's Opera was much loved in the American colonies outside stage-frightened New England, where it was not allowed to be performed until 1770, and then only in a reading, not as a staged presentation. At least one source says the gallant Nathan Hale, the Connecticut patriot fated to be hanged by the British as a spy, took part in secret readings of *The Beggar's Opera* while he was a student at Yale before the Revolution. Some Hale experts say there is no documented proof of this.

Although almost all the British soldiers of the French and Indian War would have all known *The Beggar's Opera* or its humorous songs, the rustics of New England certainly would not. If the tune to "Yankee Doodle" was related to a performance of *The Beggar's Opera,* then Shuckburgh's joke would instantly have been funny to the soldiers and their friends at Fort Crailo, but the Connecticut Yankees would have been understandably slow on the uptake.

Maverick thought the verses about the Macaroni and minding the music and step were "too good to have been produced by nameless minstrels," and that they were professionally composed. Still, he did not look deeply into a possible *Beggar's Opera* connection, nor did any of the prominent scholars.

Fort Crailo, the Van Rensselaer's Green Bush manor house, was expanded after the French and Indian War and remained in the family for generations. Today, it is a New York State historical site memorializing and interpreting Dutch culture in the Hudson Valley. Although the City of Rensselaer in which Crailo stands claims ownership of "Yankee Doodle," the state's historic site managers are more circumspect about saying the song was written there. And quite right, for myth incorrectly asserts that the *entire* song, music and words, was composed there by Shuckburgh in one blast of idle genius. The evidence that he wrote the verses to "Yankee Doodle" is only muddied by mistaken claims that he wrote the music, too, for clearly the tune had been around for generations.

One of the strongest pieces of evidence that Shuckburgh wrote verses making fun of Yankee militia at Crailo during the French and Indian War is a nineteenth-century statement by a Van Rensselaer descendant. The lady was quoted by Sonneck, who in turn excerpted from the work of historian Albert Matthews of Massachusetts: "The story of 'Yankee Doodle' is an authentic tradition in my family. My grandfather, Brig. Gen. Robert Van Rensselaer, born in the Green Bush Manor House, was a boy of seventeen at the time when Doctor Shackbergh, the writer of the verses, and General Abercrombie were guests of his father, Col. Johannes Van Rensselaer in June 1758."

Other local families, such as the Douws, claim "Dr. Shackleferd" wrote the verses on their property in 1755 during the Abercrombie campaign against Fort Ticonderoga in "derision of the four Connecticut regiments, under the command of Col. Thomas Fitch of Connecticut...."

The ill-fated James Abercrombie was not in America until 1756, however, and his failed frontal assault against the French and Indians at Ticonderoga did not take place until 1758. It is not known where Shuckburgh was in 1758, but Maverick has tracked him down to the Crailo-Albany area in 1755. There were mostly untrained militiamen in the encampments in 1755 compared with 1758, when the British Army presence numbered at least six thousand men. The glory of Johnson's 1755 victory at Lake George makes the placing of Shuckburgh's lighthearted verses in that time more logical than in 1758, when the disaster and slaughter of the Ticonderoga campaign brought only horror to the British and the colonists of New York and New England.

YANKEE DOODLE WENT TO TOWN · RIDING ON A PON

Norman Rockwell's 1937 pencil and charcoal study of Yankee Doodle for the oil painting that hangs in the Nassau Inn, Princeton, New Jersey.

What verses did Shuckburgh write? No one knows, but certainly not the ones about a "Captain Washington," who was a provincial colonel down in Virginia at the time. Or of Charles Town being burned down, which happened during the battle for Breed's Hill in 1775. Likely they were about the rustic Yankee arriving at camp, and boasting about the Cape Breton campaign. Whatever verses were first — and from the start eighteenth-century wits sitting around singing after dinner added their own — the song took on unstoppable momentum from the time of the French and Indian War.

LONG AFTER THE AMERICAN REVOLUTION and its down-to-earth heroes were sealed in plastic and turned into boring icons, Connecticut adopted a version of "Yankee Doodle" as its official state song, claiming that the original Yankee Doodle came from there.

It probably was the Connecticut militia that inspired Shuckburgh's quill at Crailo, but debate has raged over whether there was *one* particular Connecticut Yankee who was *the* doodle immortalized by the song. Naturally, that debate involves which campaign. The above-mentioned statement by the Douws regarding one Col. Thomas Fitch has been in part the basis for the Connecticut claim to being the home of the original Yankee Doodle. Was this Thomas Fitch the son of a governor, as some have said? Would the wealthy son of a governor wear chicken feathers in his hat as he marched off to war? And would he look like a country bumpkin? Whoever would believe a governor's son was just another American yokel falls victim to the same anti–New Englander prejudices the British had during colonial days and later.

Documentation about a specific Yankee Doodle leading which Connecticut militia into which campaign is lacking. One interesting note is that Revolutionary War fife music for "Yankee Doodle" was found in the archives of the Connecticut Historical Society by Kate Van Winkle Keller, who was looking for period music to play. The colonial fifer was Giles Gibbs, a militiaman from the Ellington parish, who wrote down the notes in 1777, three years before he was killed by a British-Indian raiding party in Royalton, Vt.

Connecticut folk unquestionably can claim to being the descendants of the Jankes and doedels of New Netherland scorn. The state also can be proud of its colonial militiamen, some of whom died for the sake of Dutch Yorkers in the 1690 Schenectady massacre. Many others fought bravely in the colonial wars, at least fifteen thousand in the French and Indian wars alone. Every one of them had the right to be celebrated as the original Yankee Doodle, the untrained volunteer who might have been the butt of a redcoat Yorker's joke, but whose sacrifice was crucial to the birth of the United States.

The State of Connecticut's official "Yankee Doodle" uses the famous Macaroni verse, but the "called it Macaroni" instead of "called him Macaroni." That's forgivable, as is the politically correct revision of the chorus, where Yankee Doodle is encouraged to be handy, not with the girls, but with the folks.

The feather and the macaroni verse is the best known, but for whatever reason it was not written down anywhere until 1852. Macaronies had been around in England since 1638, sometimes known to wear enormous coats, called "wrap-rascals." Well before the song "Yankee Doodle" caught the attention of redcoats, another poem entitled "The Origin of Macaronies" was quite popular; it scans perfectly for the "Yankee Doodle" words and melody. It should be questioned whether these ballad-style verses actually were sung to the same air as that of "Yankee Doodle" and might have been the inspiration for what was later sung in America. One verse is:

> *MEN with Contempt the Brutes survey'd.*
> *Nor named the silly TONIES:*
> *But WOMEN liked the Motley Breed,*
> *And called them MACARONIES.*

This Revolutionary War period verse is too nice to be from a redcoat:

> *Yankee doodle, doodle, doo,*
> *Yankee doodle dandy,*
> *All the lads and lassies are*
> *Sweet as sugar candy.*

SCHOLARS HAVE AGONIZED OVER the baffling introduction of "Uncle Sam" into Revolutionary era verses of "Yankee Doodle," since the first "Uncle Sam" is said to have been one Samuel Wilson, a Troy, N.Y., businessman who supplied beef for the army during the War of 1812. (Troy is adjacent to the City of Rensselaer and Crailo.) Wilson's beef was stamped with the government initials, "US," and it is asserted that soldiers began to say here comes the beef from Sam Wilson, or "Uncle Sam," etc. Whether Wilson had claim to being the first "Uncle Sam" is disputed, but customarily any mature black man could have been called "uncle" — as in "Uncle Tom" and "Uncle Remus."

This verse tells of a local man nicknamed "Uncle Sam," probably a free Negro, trading with the homesick militia, tired of the fare from the company mess, exchanging relatively costly molasses sugar cakes for his much-appreciated homemade food.

The first known American reference to "Yankee Doodle" as a song was in Andrew Barton's 1767 comic opera, *The Disappointment, or The Force of Credulity*. One of the songs, sung by a character named "Raccoon," which suggests a rustic bumpkin, is indicated with: Air — "Yankee Doodle":

> *O! how joyful shall I be,*
> *When I get de money,*
> *I will bring it all to dee,*
> *O! my diddling honey.*

(Exit, singing the chorus yankee doodle, etc.)

This play was about to premiere in Philadelphia in April of that year, but at the last moment it was banned by the authorities, who asserted it made fun of local personages. According to historian Grenville Vernon, "The reason for this was the fact that the action of the play had to do with the hunt for a buried treasure, and that at that moment a number of the leading citizens of Philadelphia were engaged in a similar hunt for the treasure said to have been buried by Captain Blackbeard."

THE RESPECTED MUSICOLOGIST Frank Kidson believed the "Yankee Doodle" tune was originally an air without words and was for "doodling" or "tootling" on a fife or flute. Doodling also meant to hum a tune by "deedling," "didling" or "doodling," etc. Kidson thought the best-known tune was first a favorite dance known as "The Yankee Doodle" or "The Yankee Tootle," as indicated by the words about keeping it up, minding the music and the step, and being handy with the girls. Perhaps no one person is being referred to as a Yankee doodle at all. And, of course, the dancers could hum "deedle, didle, doodle" as they danced to it.

In the 1700s, the teasing tune of "Yankee Doodle" could be used by anyone to make fun, not just by redcoats. The following was thought up to mock Benedict Arnold's wealthy mentor, Daniel Lathrop, a Yale graduate and a shrewd, though apparently opportunistic, businessman:

> *Colonel Lathrop, staunch and true,*
> *Was never known to balk it;*
> *And when he was engaged in trade*
> *He always filled his pocket.*

Lathrop was instrumental in teaching the apt young Arnold how to profit from trading in horses and from supplying armies, as well as taking part in intercolonial and overseas ventures. The sharp Yankee trader was a known personality long before the "stage Yankee" of the nineteenth century introduced the wily, dry-humored Yankee peddler into American literature as a stereotype who always brought a laugh to the audience, even in New England.

OFTEN IN THE EIGHTEENTH CENTURY, if a written work was attributed to "Anonymous," it hinted that a genteel woman was the perpetrator. Ladies of substance were not supposed to strain their delicate constitutions with the etheric fumes of high-minded writing, art, or deep thinking — though plenty did, of course, and to great effect. It is appealing to think that some of the period's rough-and-tumble political poetry — including many of those Revolutionary War verses that were set to the melody of "Yankee Doodle" — could have been the work of an otherwise demure lady.

It is even more appealing to think that those haughty fellows who were being insulted or teased by such anonymous works — the likes of Gage's mighty generals or Cornwallis or Sir Peter Parker, who lost his trousers in battle — knew only too well they were being belittled by a woman. And so did their friends and enemies.

THE SCHOLARS HAVE INVESTIGATED many possible origins for the air to "Yankee Doodle" as we know it, but the tune we know best was not the only melody that went by the name. Fife music of the period varies when it comes to playing "Yankee Doodle," the march, and there are a number of songs with "Doodle, doodle doo" for a chorus. Songs as far back as 1677 in Italy have such a chorus, and when written down for performers to follow, it was simply given as "Doodle doo, etc.," or even "Doodle, etc.," as if everyone knew what it was.

Several claims have been made to the tune of "Yankee Doodle," including Ireland, Germany, Hungary, Spain, France.... Some of those claims have come from individuals of the nineteenth century who recognized the tune from their childhood, perhaps from a familiar country dance. Maybe the tune is anciently indigenous to their hills, but it could just as well have wafted there from America decades after

"Yankee Doodle" became famous. Scholars have closely examined many claims, but none has been persuasive enough to outshine Dr. Shuckburgh's circumstantial evidence. In truth — who can really tell where an ancient melody comes from?

ROYALL TYLER, AUTHOR OF *The Contrast*, was a veteran of the Revolution, having served as aide-de-camp to General Benjamin Lincoln of Massachusetts, the man who officially received the surrender of the British at Yorktown. Tyler was born in Boston, graduated Harvard in 1776, and served through the American Revolution. He became a lawyer, practicing in Maine, then Massachusetts, and finally in Vermont, where he was chief justice of the supreme court and a professor at the University of Vermont. He is best remembered for *The Contrast* (produced in 1787) but also wrote other plays, a novel, verse, and essays. His original stage Yankee character is sometimes referred to as "Jonathan the First."

The "Yankee Doodle" verses Tyler's Jonathan recites differ slightly from the commonly known going-to-camp verses, which say "down to camp" while Tyler says "up to camp." Since he was a Revolutionary War Yankee soldier who heard the song, his version is used in Chapter Three. Furthermore, he uses, "Yankee Doodle doodle-doo" as the first line of the chorus instead of the famous "Yankee Doodle keep it up."

For the most part, the term "Yankee" indicated a rustic country-dweller, not someone from Boston or Providence or Hartford. The nickname "Yankee Doodle" is much like the period name, "Tom-a-doodle," "Tom-a-Bedlam," or "Tom fool," which like the Dutch *Jan Doedel* can mean simpleton, nitwit, half wit or fool, or even a drunk. In the case of the Yankee Doodle, he was generally a rustic from the New England back country.

Regarding the Yankee of the American popular mind after the opening of the nineteenth century, historian Francis Hodge discussed the stage Yankee so often humorously portrayed in American theater during the early 1800s: "From the first he is not a city type, who might be the same in Boston as in New York or Philadelphia, but a country fellow whose uniqueness in dress, substandard speech, and country dialect was readily discernible. He was a mixture of amiable rustic simplicity and hardy independence, with which he threw his adversaries off guard, and a shrewd and cunning intelligence, with which he unfailingly won his bargains."

After the Revolution, thousands of New Englanders migrated westward, settling throughout New York and into the Midwest. The enterprising Yankee peddler who brought his wares to trade from town to town, often on the dangerous and lawless frontier, was among the best-known characters of the period. Traveling through the North and South as well as into the distant West, the peddler was eagerly anticipated by folk who needed what he brought them, but he also carried the "reputation for hard dealing, slipperiness, and peculiar humor," said Hodge. The Yankee might seem difficult to "penetrate," but it was best not to challenge his wisdom "without first having the intelligence of also being born a Yankee."

The stage Yankee and the Yankee peddler often were looked upon as cut from the same cloth, although the first was a performer and the other a pioneer who risked his neck almost every day.

ONE THEORY ABOUT HOW Yankee and Doodle came to be stuck together is that the Puritan Yankees supposedly sang hymns incessantly, which they did through the nose — doodling, as some termed it.

Ichabod Crane, the gangly, psalm-singing schoolmaster from the 1819 Washington Irving story "The Legend of Sleepy Hollow," is another of the stereotypical portrayals of a Connecticut Yankee, in this case as viewed by a Yorker. Irving was born in New York City in 1783, so he saw first hand the heritage of the old Dutch culture, which kept such strong social and political influence in the city, even after the

Revolution. Irving's immensely popular writings shaped the thinking and tastes of his generation and of many more to come, and with his humorous *Knickerbocker's History of New York* he did even more damage to the image of the Dutch colonist than to that of the Connecticut Yankee with "The Legend of Sleepy Hollow."

The fictional Ichabod had come over the hills to live and teach in Sleepy Hollow, a Hudson Valley community of Dutch during the 1790s:

> Ichabod Crane...sojourned, or, as he expressed it, "tarried," in Sleepy Hollow, for the purpose of instructing the children of the vicinity. He was a native of Connecticut, a State which supplies the Union with pioneers for the mind as well as for the forest, and sends forth yearly its legions of frontier woodmen and country schoolmasters. The cognomen of Crane was not inapplicable to his person. He was tall, but exceedingly lank, with narrow shoulders, long arms and legs, hands that dangled a mile out of his sleeves, feet that might have served for shovels, and his whole frame most loosely hung together. His head was small, and flat at top, with huge ears, large green glassy eyes, and a long snipe nose, so that it looked like a weather-cock perched upon his spindle neck to tell which way the wind blew. To see him striding along the profile of a hill on a windy day, with his clothes bagging and fluttering about him, one might have mistaken him for the genius of famine descending upon the earth, or some scarecrow eloped from a cornfield.

The 1755 Yankee militiaman of Dr. Shuckburgh's experience is reflected in Irving's psalm-doodler, whose righteous and Puritanical sense of right and wrong is palpable as one approaches the country schoolhouse where he teaches:

From hence the low murmur of his pupils' voices, con-
ning over their lessons, might be heard in a drowsy summer's day, like the hum of a beehive; interrupted now and
then by the authoritative voice of the master, in the tone of
menace or command, or, peradventure, by the appalling
sound of the birch, as he urged some tardy loiterer along
the flowery path of knowledge. Truth to say, he was a con-
scientious man, and ever bore in mind the golden maxim,
"Spare the rod and spoil the child." Ichabod Crane's scholars
certainly were not spoiled.

I would not have it imagined, however, that he was one
of those cruel potentates of the school who joy in the smart
of their subjects; on the contrary, he administered justice
with discrimination rather than severity; taking the burden
off the backs of the weak, and laying it on those of the
strong. Your mere puny stripling, that winced at the least
flourish of the rod, was passed by with indulgence; but the
claims of justice were satisfied by inflicting a double portion on some little tough wrong-headed, broad-skirted
Dutch urchin, who sulked and swelled and grew dogged
and sullen beneath the birch. All this he called "doing his
duty by their parents;" and he never inflicted a chastise-
ment without following it by the assurance, so consolatory
to the smarting urchin, that "he would remember it and
thank him for it the longest day he had to live."

If Irving's potent pen immortalized the cartoon version of the
Yankee singing master, it positively demolished the reality of the
adventurous, stronghearted colonists from many lands who came to
New Netherland and challenged the eastern wilderness when few
Europeans had ventured more than five miles from home. Irving's
"Legend of Sleepy Hollow" was supposedly found in the papers of a fat
old Dutchman, Diedrich Knickerbocker, an indolent, pipe-smoking

oaf, comfortable in his easy chair, served hand and foot by his good, plump *vrouw*.

Pretending to be working from these papers, Irving created *Knickerbocker's History of New York,* in which he excruciatingly, character-assassinatingly describes Wouter van Twiller, one of the first governors of New Amsterdam. In reality young, dynamic, and innovative, Van Twiller is described by Irving as a "renowned old gentleman" who was "descended from a long line of Dutch burgomasters, who had successively dozed away their lives and grown fat upon the bench of magistracy in Rotterdam...." The real Van Twiller, who feathered his own nest but was trusted by the Indians, was expert in livestock and the nurturing of orchards and staple grains — for which, thanks to him, New York was famous decades after. Even the native tribes took Dutch fruits and vegetables as their own and brought them home to cultivate.

Irving described Van Twiller as an old dullard and an enormously fat one, although he was actually young and slim. Irving's Van Twiller concealed his ignorance by seldom speaking, and he was tranquilly unconcerned about "the perplexities of the world. He had lived in it for years without feeling the least curiosity to know whether the sun revolved around it, or it around the sun; and he had watched, for at least half a century, the smoke curling from his pipe to the ceiling, without once troubling his head with any of those numerous theories by which a philosopher would have perplexed his brain, in accounting for its rising above the surrounding atmosphere."

Thus did the influential Irving tickle his American readers, and thus did he plant the notion in their minds that the Dutch colonials were all fat men with fat wives and no imagination or ambition whatsoever and of no consequence in the progress of Anglo-America, which the English-speakers were willing to believe. Recounting in *Knickerbocker's History* the colonial conflicts between the "lean and hungry Yankees" and the indolent Dutch wreathed in clouds of tobacco smoke that were like an "impenetrable fog," Irving even went so far as to mock the dashing Arent van Curler.

Irving, the effete Manhattan socialite, called this fearless soldier of fortune a "jolly, robustious trumpeter…famous for his long wind." Van Curler, he who laughed and bared his behind at Indian demons, would have mooned Irving, too — Irving and all those suave, English-bred New Yorkers of the early nineteenth century who could not imagine that Dutch colonists were rough, tough personalities — men and women, both. The multi-ethnic colonists of New Netherland stood it out against all the odds, fought Indians and roved abroad with them, were virtually abandoned by the Company that owned them, and still came back to recover New Amsterdam, which they briefly renamed New Orange, only to have the *verdommte* home government abandon them, too.

Irving's New Netherlanders describe the encroaching Yankees as a "squatting, bundling, guessing, questioning, swapping, pumpkin-eating, molasses-daubing, shingle-splitting, cider-watering, horse-jockeying, notion-peddling crew…." Here, he might not have been far off about how the Dutch saw Connecticut folk. Otherwise, however, *Knickerbocker's* best-selling, closely studied, delightfully witty — and unfortunately believed — *History of New York* consigned the vigorous and aspiring Dutch colonial initiative in America to the realm of adorable folklore and whimsy. How Irving maligned Pieter Stuyvesant says more about the vapidity of New York Knickerbockers, as Irving's type were termed, than about that potent seventeenth-century American colonist who was a father to infant New York.

Little wonder that Irving-smitten nineteenth-century America could not fathom the depth of hostility between New Netherland and New England, and so could not feel the intense sting of the term "Yankee Doodle." By the turn of the twentieth century, when Oscar Sonneck did his "Yankee Doodle" research for the Library of

Congress, Irving's sedentary New York Dutchman and goofy Connecticut Yankee were too firmly planted in the popular mind.

Throughout the first half of the nineteenth century, various renditions of "Yankee Doodle" came and went, among them "Yankee Doodle in Mexico," during the Mexican wars of the 1840s. Instead of Brother Jonathan, the Yankee was named Uncle Sam, a self-righteous campaigner carrying forth the banner of "Manifest Destiny."

> *To Mexico went Uncle Sam*
> *To trade and then to settle,*
> *But found the government as harsh*
> *As its emblazoned nettle.*

> *Yankee Doodle came to town*
> *Peaceably, you knew it,*
> *But you dared to insult his flag,*
> *And he made you rue it.*

One of the American heroes of that conflict was General Zachary Taylor, who was lauded in another version:

> *There's not a heart in all the land,*
> *That beats not firm and steady,*
> *For the hero of the Rio Grande,*
> *Old gallant Rough and Ready.*

> *His foes may slander as they can,*
> *And bluster at his manners.*
> *Who cares a fig? He's just the man*
> *To lead the Yankee Banners.*

As the United States grew away from colonial and Revolutionary days, there developed a longing to recall past glory, and the meaning of "Yankee Doodle" was sought for by many a scholar and researcher. The old melody continued to inspire songwriters to renew it in their own way, and about 1855 popular songwriter George P. Morris wrote "The Origin of Yankee Doodle," calling the British government "Johnny Bull," and evoking the popular notion of what the Revolution was all about:

Once on a time old Johnny Bull flew in a raging fury,
And swore that Jonathan should have no trials, sir, by jury.
That no elections should be held across the briny waters:
And now, said he, "I'll tax the tea of all his sons and daughters."
Then down he sate in burly state, and blustered like a grandee,
And in derision made a tune call'd "Yankee doodle dandy."
"Yankee doodle" — these are facts — "Yankee doodle dandy:
My son of wax, your tea I'll tax; you — Yankee doodle dandy."
John sent the tea from o'er the sea, with heavy duties rated;
But whether hyson or bohea, I never heard it stated.
Then Jonathan to pout began — he laid a strong embargo —
"I'll drink no TEA, by Jove," so he threw overboard the cargo.
When Johnny sent a regiment, big words and looks to bandy,
Whose martial band, when near the land, play'd "Yankee doodle dandy."
"Yankee doodle — keep it up — Yankee doodle dandy —
I'll poison with a tax your cup; you — Yankee doodle dandy."

"Yankee Doodle" became the march to which John Bull's soldiers retreated, and Jonathan came to like it: "'That tune,' says he, 'suits to a T. I'll sing it ever after.'" The final chorus mingles the dandy and doodle-doo versions:

Yankee doodle, firm and true — Yankee doodle dandy —
Yankee doodle, doodle doo, Yankee doodle dandy.

THERE WERE NEW VERSIONS of "Yankee Doodle" during the Civil War, from both North and South. One was "Yankee Doodle for Lincoln."

> *Yankee Doodle does as well*
> *As anybody can, sir,*
> *And like the ladies, he's for Abe,*
> *And Union to a man, sir.*

Confederates equated themselves with the colonial patriots revolting against a tyrannical government. As such, they erected liberty poles and sang versions of "Yankee Doodle" that expressed their bitterness against Northerners, all of whom they lumped under the name "Yankees."

> *Yankee Doodle had a mind*
> *To whip the Southern "traitors,"*
> *Because they didn't choose to live*
> *On codfish and potatoes.*

The chorus changes each time, playing with the notion of all Northerners, including Abraham Lincoln, being drunkards.

> *Yankee Doodle, doodle doo,*
> *Yankee Doodle dandy,*
> *And so to keep his courage up*
> *He took a drink of brandy.*

Confederate soldiers were called "Johnny Rebel," or "Johnnies," while the Federals were called "Billy Yank," or just plain "Yankees." Which also means Johnnies.

The Civil War era produced perhaps the most beautiful arrangement of the melody of "Yankee Doodle," composed by New Orleans–born pianist Louis Moreau Gottschalk as part of a larger piece entitled *The Union*. Gottschalk was the son of an English-German father and an aristocratic Creole mother, and was a Southerner who stayed loyal to the Federal government. A prodigy, he studied in Europe and then returned to tour the United States and dazzle his audiences. Performing *The Union* in a Washington, D.C., concert in the early days of national dissension, he thrilled President Lincoln and his entourage, but the many pro-secession Southerners in the audience sat on their hands during the applause.

During the war years, Gottschalk gave concerts throughout the Federal-held regions, at times just a few hours ahead of a battle. Playing the old-fashioned and well-worn "Yankee Doodle" always appealed to the people, he said, but it was certain to stir up complaints from the pseudo-sophisticated critics in the audience. After watching a violinist perform in Springfield, Ill., he wrote in his memoirs: "Doehler plays 'Yankee Doodle' and [Gottschalk's own] *Carnival of Venice*, two pieces that never fail in exciting the enthusiasm of the audience, but that invariably next day bring out a severe lecture from the newspapers. Fortunately we know what to think of it. It is only to save appearances that these gentlemen protest. They like this trivial music secretly, but like all those who are conscious of their inferiority, they wish to conceal it by openly affecting to despise what secretly they love."

SETTINGS AND ADAPTATIONS OF "Yankee Doodle" continued to appear. While visiting the United States in the 1870s, Russian pianist Anton Rubinstein wrote a set of thirty-nine variations; in 1893 the Czech composer Anton Dvorak included it in his *Symphony No. 9 (From the New World)*. In the first part of the twentieth century the zany Marx Brothers performed a song called "Monkey Doodle-doo," written by Irving Berlin. The best-known adaptation of all is "Yankee Doodle Boy," by Broadway songwriter George M. Cohan, a native Rhode Islander. Styled "The Yankee Doodle comedian," Cohan took every opportunity to wave the American flag (often with "Yankee" or "Yankee Doodle" in the title of his songs or plays). Perhaps even better known than the original "Yankee Doodle," Cohan's "Yankee Doodle Boy," sometimes called "Yankee Doodle Dandy," was the hit song in a biographical film about him, and starring James Cagney.

One of the first historians of old New York was the well-regarded John Pintard, a former Revolutionary War soldier who tried to get to the bottom of the "Yankee Doodle" story. Pintard's papers regarding this study have been lost, unfortunately, but in 1789 he wrote to Massachusetts historian and clergyman Jeremy Belknap: "I am attempting to collect the scattered members of Yankee doodle to see how far it has hitherto been spun out. I consider the different wars of America as the several epochs of its continuation. How far back it reaches or which is the Alpha of this endless song you may enable me to trace out. But I am inclined to suppose it will be found of the nature of the Pirate's signature when each person wrote his name in a circle, which of course had neither beginning nor end."

Not yet.

I'm a Yankee Doodle Dandy,
A Yankee Doodle do or die.
A real live nephew of my Uncle Sam's,
Born on the Fourth of July.

I've got a Yankee Doodle sweetheart,
She's my Yankee Doodle joy —

Yankee Doodle came to London
Just to ride a pony —
I am that Yankee Doodle Boy!

ACKNOWLEDGMENTS

The author is sincerely grateful to all those who so generously contributed their time and expertise. What is right in this book is largely thanks to them and also to those scholars — especially Oscar G. Sonneck, first head of the Music Division of the Library of Congress — who over the years so diligently pursued the origins of "Yankee Doodle" and left a bright legacy for our benefit.

First, thanks to Marian and Robert Guerriero, who saw the importance of telling the story of America's song, and without whose encouragement this book would not have been possible.

A special thanks to Paul R. Huey, scientist (archaeology) at the New York State Bureau of Historic Sites, who generously shared his many years of research into the life and lineage of Dr. Richard Shuckburgh, traveled to Warwickshire, England, to meet the Shuckburgh family, and was an inspiration for this book.

I am grateful to editor Sarah Novak, whose deft and professional touch has once again been so indispensable; to Ron Toelke and Barbara Kempler-Toelke of Ron Toelke Associates, book designers who know how to work with an author; and to Collins Sennett, who does so much so well behind the scenes.

Again thanks to the staff of the Chatham, New York, Public Library for their kindness and help: Wendy Fuller, director; Carolyn Brust, and Elizabeth Gaupman. Thanks to Katharine Westwood, supervisor of local history and genealogy at the Berkshire Athenaeum, Pittsfield, Mass.

The author is grateful for the valuable advice of Revolutionary War experts George Neumann and Ray Andrews, and also to Mark Nichipor of the Minute Man National Historic Park, Concord, Mass., and to Mary Ellen Grimaldi, historic site assistant at Crailo State Historic Site, Rensselaer, N.Y.

Thanks for his kind assistance to Dutch author Henri van der Zee, who with his English wife, Barbara, have brought New Netherland to life as few other writers ever have; the Van der Zees have shown how much more there is to colonial America when the Dutch are properly accounted for.

Sincere thanks to Christopher D. Campbell, professor at the University of Virginia and an expert on *The Beggar's Opera*, whose Internet website was so extremely helpful. Thanks to Mary Campbell of the Johns Hopkins University Library for her special effort to see that the author had all the words of a "Yankee Doodle" version and also that a lecture by Lester S. Levy was included in the author's research.

Thanks again to Thomas Rockwell and the Norman Rockwell Trust, and to Pamela A. Mendelsohn, curatorial assistant of the Norman Rockwell Museum at Stockbridge; also to Mary Seitz Pagano of the Norman Rockwell Estate Licensing Company. Thanks to Elizabeth Appleby of the Delaware Art Museum, for her advice on the work of artist Howard Pyle.

Thanks for help with other images to Jenna Loosemore, curatorial assistant at the American Antiquarian Society, to Elsie Maddaus, archivist and librarian at Schenectady County Historical Society, and to Ann Sindelar, reference supervisor at Western Reserve Historical Society Library. Also thanks to C.W. Spangenberger for the loan of a fine old book that had the illustration of Crailo; also to Ramades Suarez of the print department of New York Public Library.

Thanks to Kathy Johnson, a devoted student of the Dutch in New Netherland; also to Danelle Moon, reference manager of Yale University Library, and to Warder Cadbury for his timely and excellent suggestions in searching for "Yankee Doodle" broadsides. Also thanks to Mary Ortner, for information on Nathan Hale, and likewise to Martha Smart of the Connecticut Historical Society, Al Palko of the Connecticut State Library, and Robert G. Babcock and Vincent Giroud of the Yale University Library.

Particular thanks to Aaron Murray and Jeremy Murray for considerable legwork in New York City and Albany libraries.

As ever and with all the books, this one required the support and advice of my Dutch wife, Els Murray-van Dijk, who knows "Yankee Doodle" is *Janke Doedel*.

Thanks, finally, to Tordis Ilg Isselhardt, publisher of Images from the Past, who saw here the story that others could not see.

SELECT BIBLIOGRAPHY

Anburey, Thomas. *Travels through the Interior Parts of America*. Boston: Houghton Mifflin, 1923.

Apel, Willi. *Harvard Dictionary of Music*. Cambridge, Mass.: Harvard University Press, 1944.

Balcom, B.A. "Louisbourg." Article published by the website of the Fortress of Louisbourg National Historic Site, Cape Breton Island, Nova Scotia.

Bird, Harrison. *March to Saratoga*. New York: Oxford University Press, 1963.

Bliven, Bruce, Jr. *Under the Guns: New York: 1775-1776*. New York: Harper & Row, Publishers, 1972.

Browne, C.A. *The Story of Our National Ballads*. New York: Thomas Y. Crowell Company, 1931.

Burke, Thomas E. *Mohawk Frontier*. Ithaca and London: Cornell University Press, 1991.

Callahan, North. *Royal Raiders*. New York: Bobbs-Merrill, 1963.

Cavanaugh, John. "In Norwalk, Yankee Doodle Spurs a Dandy of a Debate." *New York Times,* March 18, 1984.

Chidsey, Donald Barr. *The Loyalists*. New York: Crown Publishers, 1973.

Commager, Henry S. and Richard Morris, eds. *The Spirit of Seventy-six*. New York: Harper & Row, 1974.

Damon, S. Foster. *Yankee Doodle*. Providence: Brown University, 1959.

Daniels, Bruce. *Puritans at Play*. New York: St. Martin's Press, 1995.

Davis, Burke. *The Campaign that Won America*. New York: The Dial Press, 1970.

Diamant, Lincoln. *Yankee Doodle Days*. Fleischmanns, N.Y.: Purple Mountain Press, 1996.

Dorson, Richard M. *America in Legend*. New York: Pantheon Books, 1973.

Dunn, Richard S. *Puritans and Yankees*. New York: W.W. Norton, 1962.

Edmonds, Walter D. *The Musket and the Cross*. Boston: Little, Brown and Company, 1968.

Elson, Louis Charles. *The National Music of America and Its Sources*. Boston: L.C. Page and Company, 1900.

Ewen, David, ed. *Songs of America*. Westport, Conn.: Greenwood Press, Publishers, 1978.

Falkner, Leonard. *Forge of Liberty*. New York: E.P. Dutton & Co., 1959.

Fellows, Larry. "Yankee Doodle Still a Dandy." *Darien News,* March 15, 1984, Darien, Conn.

Fischer, David Hackett. *Paul Revere's Ride*. New York: Oxford University Press, 1994.

Fiske, John. *The American Revolution*, 2 Vols. Boston & New York: Houghton, Mifflin & Company, 1891.

Fleming, Thomas J. *Beat the Last Drum: The Siege of Yorktown, 1781*. New York: St. Martin's Press, 1963.

Forcucci, Samuel L. *A Folk Song History of America*. Englewood Cliffs, N.J.: Prentice-Hall, 1984.

Fuld, James J. *The Book of World-Famous Music: Classical, Popular and Folk*. New York: Dover, 1995.

Furneaux, Rupert. *The Pictorial History of the American Revolution*. Chicago: J.G. Ferguson Publishing Company, 1973.

Galvin, John R. *Three Men of Boston*. New York: Thomas Y. Crowell Company, 1976.

Griffis, William Elliot. *The Story of New Netherland*. Boston and New York: Houghton Mifflin Company, 1909.

Griffith, Benjamin W., Jr., ed. *The Beggar's Opera* by John Gay. Great Neck, N.Y.: Barron's Educational Series, 1962.

Hamilton, Alexander. *Itinerarium*. New York: Arno Press & The New York Times, 1971.

Hornblow, Arthur. *A History of Theater in America,* 2 Vols. New York: Benjamin Blom, 1965.

Howard, J.T. *Our American Music,* 4th edition. New York: T.Y. Crowell Co., 1965.

Irving, Washington. *Knickerbocker's History of New York*. New York: Doubleday, Doran & Company, 1928.

Janvier, Thomas A. *The Dutch Founding of New York*. Port Washington, N.Y.: Ira J. Friedman, 1903.

Jennings, John. *Boston, Cradle of Liberty*. Garden City, N.Y.: Doubleday & Company, 1947.

Kammen, Michael. *Colonial New York*. New York: Charles Scribner's Sons, 1975.

Kelley, S.J. "The Spirit of '76." *The Clevelander Magazine,* (Nov. 1938), 23.

Kenney, Alice P. *Stubborn for Liberty: The Dutch in New York*. Syracuse: Syracuse University Press, 1975.

Ketchum, Richard M., ed. *The Revolution*. New York: American Heritage Publishing Company, 1958.

Kidson, Frank. *The Beggar's Opera: Its Predecessors and Successors*. London: Cambridge University Press, 1922.

Leach, Douglas Edward. *The Northern Colonial Frontier, 1607-1763*. New York: Holt Rhinehart and Winston, 1966.

Lehman, Pamela A. "The Schenectady Massacre." Schenectady Historical Society, Schenectady, N.Y., 1972.

LeMay, Leo J. "The American Origins of 'Yankee Doodle.'" *William & Mary Quarterly,* 1976, Vol. 33, 435-464.

Levy, Lester S. "Yankee Doodle." A lecture. Lester S. Levy Collection of Sheet Music at the Milton Eisenhower Library, Johns Hopkins University, Baltimore.

Lester S. Levy Collection of Sheet Music at the Milton Eisenhower Library, Johns Hopkins University, Baltimore.

Lossing, Benson J. *The Pictorial Field-book of the American Revolution*. New York: Harper & Brothers, 1860.

Madden, Richard. "A Song for Connecticut: Macaroni or Oak Tree?" *New York Times,* February 17, 1984.

Mates, Julian. *The American Musical Stage Before 1800*. New Brunswick: Rutgers University Press, 1962.

Maverick, Lewis A. "Yankee Doodle." *The American Neptune,* Vol. 22, No. 2 (April, 1962), 106-135.

Moore, Frank. *Songs and Ballads of the American Revolution.* New York: D. Appleton & Co. 1856.

Munsell, Joel. *The Annals of Albany,* Vol 2. Albany: Joel Munsell, 1870.

Murray, Stuart. *The Honor of Command — General Burgoyne's Saratoga Campaign.* Bennington: Images from the Past, 1998.

O'Callaghan, E.B. *The Documentary History of the State of New York,* Vols. 1 and 8. Albany. Weed, Parsons & Co., 1850.

Opie, Peter and Iona. *The Oxford Dictionary of Nursery Rhymes.* New York: Clarendon Press, 1951.

Parkman, Francis. *France and England in North America.* New York: Frederick Ungar Publishing Company, 1965.

Rabson, Carolyn. *Songbook of the American Revolution.* Peaks Island, Me.: NEO Press, 1974.

Randall, Willard Sterne. *Benedict Arnold.* New York: Quill, 1990.

Roberts, Edgar V., ed. and John Gay. *The Beggar's Opera.* Lincoln, Nebraska: University of Nebraska Press, 1969.

Rutledge, Joseph L. and Thomas B. Costain, ed. *Century of Conflict.* New York: Doubleday & Company, 1956.

Scholes, Percy A. *Oxford Companion to Music.* London: Oxford University Press, 1965.

Silber, Irwin. *Songs of Independence.* Harrisburg: Stackpole Books, 1973.

Singleton, Esther. *Dutch New York.* New York: Dodd, Mead and Company, 1909.

Slonimsky, Nicolas, ed. *Baker's Biographical Dictionary of Musicians.* New York: Schirmer Books, 1984.

Schmalz, Jeffrey. "Norwalk Historians Argue the Reality of Yankee Doodle." *New York Times,* April 19, 1984.

Sonneck, Oscar G. *Report on "The Star-Spangled Banner," "Hail Columbia," "America," and "Yankee Doodle."* Washington, D.C.: Library of Congress, 1909.

Van der Donck, Adriaen. *A Description of New Netherlands.* Syracuse: Syracuse University Press, 1968.

Van der Zee, Henri and Barbara. *A Sweet and Alien Land: The Story of Dutch New York.* New York: The Viking Press, 1978.

Vernon, Grenville. *Yankee Doodle-doo, A Collection of Songs of the Early American Stage.* New York: Payson & Clarke, 1927.

Winstock, Lewis. *Music and Songs of the Redcoats, 1642-1902.* Harrisburg: Stackpole Books, 1970.

SOURCES OF ILLUSTRATIONS

Cover: The Western Reserve Historical Society, Cleveland, Ohio

Frontispiece: Courtesy, American Antiquarian Society

x, 3, 15, 18: *The History of Our Country* Vol.1, Edward S. Ellis, The Jones Brothers Publishing Co., Cincinnati and Henry W. Knight, New York, 1895

10, 29, 59, 62-63, 66-67, 73, 92-93, 97, 118, 160-161, 168-169: Various sources including *The Life and Times of Washington,* J.F. Schroeder, Johnson Fry and Co., New York, 1857 and *The American Revolution* Vol. 1, John Fiske, Houghton, Mifflin & Co., Boston and New York, 1896

22-23, 35: *The Documentary History of the State of New York,* Vol. IV, E.B. O'Callaghan, Charles Van Benthuysen, Public Printer, Albany, 1851

46-47, 50-51: Schenectady County Historical Society

79, 85: *Catchpenny Prints: 163 Popular Engravings from the Eighteenth Century,* Dover Publications, Inc., New York, 1970

98, 102-103, 110-111, 114, 128-129, 132-133, 138-139, 150-151, 165, 186: *The American Revolution: A Picture Sourcebook,* John Grafton, Dover Publications, Inc., New York, 1975

182-183: Beverley R. Robinson Collection, U.S. Naval Academy, Annapolis, Maryland

192: Print Collection, Miriam and Ira D. Wallach Division of Art, Prints and Photographs, The New York Public Library

204-205: Photo courtesy of The Norman Rockwell Museum at Stockbridge. Reproduced courtesy of the Norman Rockwell Family Trust.

Index

IMAGES FROM THE PAST
Publishing history in ways that help people see it for themselves

Other books by Stuart Murray

RUDYARD KIPLING IN VERMONT: Birthplace of The Jungle Books

This book fills a gap in the biographical coverage of the important British author who is generally described as having lived only in India and England. It provides the missing links in the bittersweet story that haunts the portals of Naulakha, the distinctive shingle-style home built by Kipling and his American wife near Brattleboro, Vermont. Here the Kiplings lived for four years and the first two of their three children were born.

All but one of Kipling's major works stem from these years of rising success, happiness and productivity.

6" x 9", 208 pages; extensive index. Excerpts from Kipling poems, 21 historical photos; 6 book illustrations; and 7 sketches.

ISBN 1-884592-04-X Cloth $29.00 ISBN 1-884592-05-8 Paperback $18.95

THE HONOR OF COMMAND: Gen. Burgoyne's Saratoga Campaign

Leaving Quebec in June, Burgoyne was confident in his ability to strike a decisive blow against the rebellion in the colonies. Instead, the stubborn rebels fought back, slowed his advance and inflicted irreplaceable losses, leading to his defeat and surrender at Saratoga on October 17, 1777 — an important turning point in the American Revolution. Burgoyne's point of view as the campaign progresses is expressed from his dispatches, addresses to his army, and exchanges with friends and fellow officers.

7" x 10", 128 pages; 33 prints and engravings, 8 maps, 10 sketches. Index.
ISBN 1-884-592-03-1 Paperback $14.95

NORMAN ROCKWELL AT HOME IN VERMONT:
The Arlington Years, 1939-1953

Norman Rockwell painted some of his greatest works, including "The Four Freedoms" during the 15 years he and his family lived in Arlington, Vermont. Compared to his former home in the suburbs of New York City, it was "like living in another world," and completely transformed his already successful career as America's leading illustrator. For the first time he began to paint pictures that "grew out of the every day life of my neighbors."

7" x 10", 96 pages; 32 historical photographs, 13 Rockwell paintings and sketches, and personal recollections. Index. Regional map, selected bibliography, and listing of area museums and exhibitions.

ISBN 1-884592-02-3 Paperback $14.95

WASHINGTON'S FAREWELL: The Final Parting With His Officers After Victory in the Revolution

The story of George Washington's emotional parting with his most loyal officers on December 4, 1783, just days after final victory in the Revolution. In a moving and utterly silent occasion at Fraunces Tavern in New York City, officer after officer crosses the room to shake Washington's hand and bid their beloved commander goodbye. The story of each man's exploits in the war is vividly recounted in a patchwork of vignettes that capture the triumph and drama of the war they waged for liberty. Illustrated with period art.

5" x 7", 248 pages; 35 visuals. Notes. Index. ISBN 1-884592-20-1 Cloth $21.00

Other Images from the Past books

ALLIGATORS ALWAYS DRESS FOR DINNER: An Alphabet Book of Vintage Photographs

By Linda Donigan and Michael Horwitz

A collection of late 19th- and early 20th-century images reproduced in rich duotone for children and all who love historical photographs. Each two-page spread offers a surprising visual treat: Beholding Beauty — a beautifully dressed and adorned Kikuyu couple; Fluted Fingers — a wandering Japanese Zen monk playing a bamboo recorder; and Working the Bandwagon — the Cole Brothers Band on an elaborate 1879 circus wagon. A-Z information pages with image details send readers back for another look.

9 1/4" x 9 3/4", 64 pages ISBN 1-884592-08-2 Cloth $25.00

LETTERS TO VERMONT Volumes I and II: From Her Civil War Soldier Correspondents to the Home Press

Donald Wickman, Editor/Compiler

In their letters "To the Editor" of the Rutland Herald, young Vermont soldiers tell of fighting for the Union, galloping around Lee's army in Virginia, garrisoning the beleaguered defenses of Washington, D.C., and blunting Pickett's desperate charge at Gettysburg. One writer is captured, another serves as a prison camp guard, others are wounded — and one dies fighting in the horrific conflict in the Wilderness of Virginia. Biographical information for each writer (except one who remains an enigma) and supporting commentary on military affairs. 54 engravings and prints, 32 contemporary maps, 45 historical photographs. Extensive index.

Vol. 1, 6" x 9", 251 pages ISBN 1-884592-10-4 Cloth $30.00 ISBN 1-884592-11-2 Paper $19.95

Vol. 2, 6" x 9", 265 pages ISBN 1-884592-16-3 Cloth $30.00 ISBN 1-884592-17-1 Paper $19.95

REMEMBERING GRANDMA MOSES

By Beth Moses Hickok

Grandma Moses, a crusty, feisty, upstate New York farm wife and grandmother, as remembered in affectionate detail by Beth Moses Hickok, who married into the family at 22, and raised two of Grandma's granddaughters. Set in 1934, before the artist was "discovered," the book includes family snapshots, and photographs that evoke the landscape of Eagle Bridge, home for most of her century-plus life. Two portraits of Grandma Moses — a 1947 painting and a 1949 photograph, and nine historical photographs. On the cover is a rare colorful yarn painting given to the author as a wedding present. 6" x 9", 64 pages ISBN 1-884592-01-5 $12.95

Available at your local bookstore or from Images from the Past, Inc., 888-442-3204 for credit card orders; P.O. Box 137, Bennington, Vermont 05201 with check or money order. When ordering, please add $4.00 shipping and handling for the first book and $1 for each additional. (Add 5% sales tax for shipments to Vermont.)